PREFACE.

An earnest wish having been expressed by my Publishers that this new Edition of the Irish Melodies should be accompanied by a few prefatory words, I have readily yielded to their request; though so frequently have I been called to this very welcome task, that all I can say upon such a theme, without degenerating into mere needless egotism, must have been long since exhausted.

On the poetical part of this work, it is not for me to give an opinion. Whatever may be its merits, to the music they are almost solely owing. It was, indeed, my strong desire to convey in words some of those feelings and fancies which music seemed to me to utter that first led me to attempt poetry. Thus song was the inspiring medium through which I became initiated into verse. Whatever merit there may be in interpreting the voice that spoke in my country's music, lending it a vent in verse, and bringing home to other hearts besides my own the various feelings, sad, gay, or impassioned, with which it teems, to such merit I may, perhaps, proudly pretend. But the whole source and soul of the IRISH MELODIES lies in their matchless music. As I have already said in song, I was only as the wind to the sleeping harp, and "all the wild sweetness I waked was its own."

I shall only add, that I deem it most fortunate for this new Edition that the rich, imaginative powers of Mr. MACLISE have been employed in its adornment; and that, to complete its national character, an Irish pencil has lent its aid to an Irish pen in rendering due honour and homage to our country's ancient harp.

THOMAS MOORE.

₊ *The designs are in facsimile of the original drawings, and the text is engraved by Mr. Becker's process.*

Moore's Irish Melodies
The Illustrated 1846 Edition

Thomas Moore

Illustrated by
DANIEL MACLISE

DOVER PUBLICATIONS, INC.
Mineola, New York

Moore's Irish Melodies
The Illustrated 1846 Edition

Thomas Moore

Illustrated by
DANIEL MACLISE

DOVER PUBLICATIONS, INC.
Mineola, New York

Copyright

Copyright © 2000 by Dover Publications, Inc.
All rights reserved under Pan American and International Copyright Conventions.

Published in Canada by General Publishing Company, Ltd., 30 Lesmill Road, Don Mills, Toronto, Ontario.

Bibliographical Note

This Dover edition, first published in 2000, is a complete and unabridged republication of the work originally published by Longman, Brown, Green, and Longmans, London, 1846. The Publisher's Note is newly added. The original frontispiece and half-title are reproduced on the inside cover of this edition.

DOVER *Pictorial Archive* SERIES

This book belongs to the Dover Pictorial Archive Series. You may use the designs and illustrations for graphics and crafts applications, free and without special permission, provided that you include no more than ten in the same publication or project. (For permission for additional use, please write to Permissions Department, Dover Publications, Inc., 31 East 2nd Street, Mineola, N.Y. 11501.)

However, republication or reproduction of any illustration by any other graphic service, whether it be in a book or in any other design resource, is strictly prohibited.

Library of Congress Cataloging-in-Publication Data

Moore, Thomas, 1779–1852.
    [Irish melodies]
    Moore's Irish melodies : the illustrated 1846 edition / Thomas Moore ; illustrated by Daniel Maclise.
        p. cm. — (Dover pictorial archive series)
    Originally published: London : Longman, Brown, Green, and Longmans, 1846.
    "The original frontispiece and half-title are reproduced on the inside cover of this edition"—T.P. verso.
    ISBN 0-486-41101-X
    1. Nationalism—Ireland—Poetry. 2. Ireland—Poetry. I. Title: Irish melodies. II. Maclise, Daniel, 1806–1870. III. Title. IV. Series.

PR5054 .I8 2000
821'.7—dc21

99-057798

Manufactured in the United States of America
Dover Publications, Inc., 31 East 2nd Street, Mineola, N.Y. 11501

Publisher's Note

Poet, satirist, composer, musician, Irish patriot, and friend of Byron and Shelley, THOMAS MOORE (1779–1852) published twelve *Irish Melodies* in 1807—the first of ten installments of over 100 national song lyrics that would occupy him for almost three decades, until their completion in 1834. Considered his major poetic work, the *Melodies* were set to his own music and that of Sir John Stevenson, and performed by the poet himself for London's aristocracy, arousing sympathy and support for the Irish nationalists, among whom Moore was a national hero.

DANIEL MACLISE (1806–1870)—Ireland's illustrious and greatly honored graduate and, later, official academician of the Royal Academy—provided the delicate, fanciful artwork for the 1846 edition of Moore's collected *Melodies*. Noted as one of his country's foremost history painters, Maclise was warmly acknowledged by Moore for his imaginative contributions . . . "an Irish pencil has lent its aid to an Irish pen in rendering the honour and homage to our country's ancient harp." (*from the Preface to the 1846 edition*).

Go where glory waits thee,
But while fame elates thee,
    Oh! still remember me.
When the praise thou meetest
To thine ear is sweetest,
    Oh! then remember me.

Other arms may press thee,
Dearer friends caress thee,
All the joys that bless thee,
   Sweeter far may be;
But when friends are nearest,
And when joys are dearest,
   Oh! then remember me!

When, at eve, thou rovest
By the star thou lovest,
   Oh! then remember me.
Think, when home returning,
Bright we've seen it burning,
   Oh! thus remember me.
Oft as summer closes,
When thine eye reposes
On its ling'ring roses,
   Once so lov'd by thee,
Think of her who wove them,
Her who made thee love them,
   Oh! then remember me.

When, around thee dying,
Autumn leaves are lying,
   Oh! then remember me.
And, at night, when gazing
On the gay hearth blazing,
   Oh! still remember me,
Then should music, stealing
All the soul of feeling,
To thy heart appealing,
   Draw one tear from thee;
Then let memory bring thee
Strains I us'd to sing thee,—
   Oh! then remember me.

Remember Thee.

Remember thee? yes, while there's life in this heart,
It shall never forget thee, all lorn as thou art;
More dear in thy sorrow, thy gloom, and thy showers,
Than the rest of the world in their sunniest hours.

Wert thou all that I wish thee, great, glorious, and free,
First flower of the earth, and first gem of the sea,
I might hail thee with prouder, with happier brow,
But oh! could I love thee more deeply than now?

No, thy chains as they rankle, thy blood as it runs,
But make thee more painfully dear to thy sons—
Whose hearts, like the young of the desert-bird's nest,
Drink love in each life-drop that flows from thy breast.

Erin, thy silent tear never shall cease,
Erin, thy languid smile ne'er shall increase,
Till, like the rainbow's light,
Thy various tints unite,
And form in heaven's sight
One arch of peace!

Oh! breathe not his Name.

Oh! breathe not his name, let it sleep in the shade,
Where cold and unhonour'd his relics are laid:
Sad, silent, and dark, be the tears that we shed,
As the night-dew that falls on the grass o'er his head.

But the night-dew that falls, though in silence it weeps,
Shall brighten with verdure the grave where he sleeps;
And the tear that we shed, though in secret it rolls,
Shall long keep his memory green in our souls.

D. Maclise, R.A. F. P. Becker.

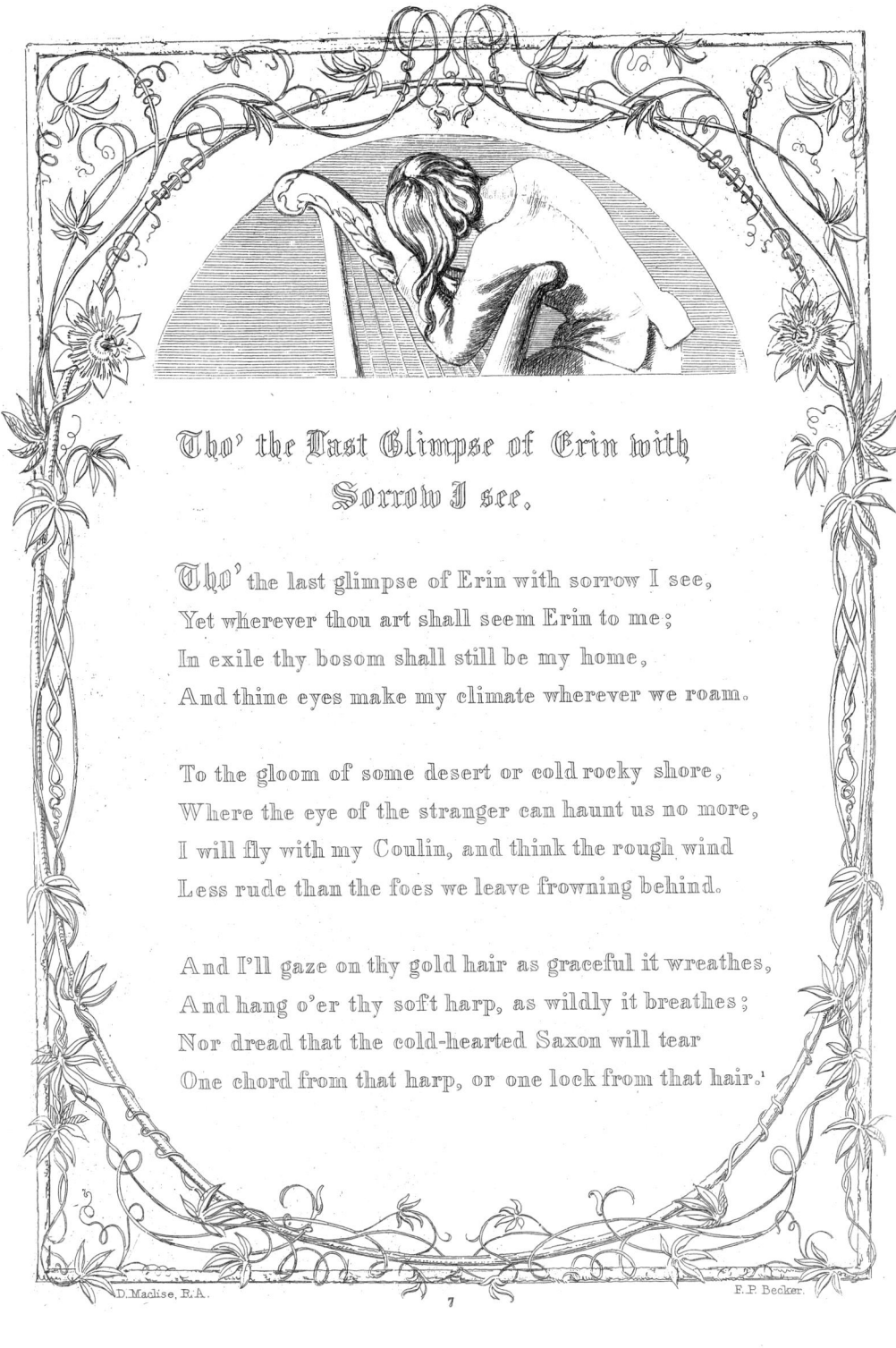

Tho' the Last Glimpse of Erin with Sorrow I see.

Tho' the last glimpse of Erin with sorrow I see,
Yet wherever thou art shall seem Erin to me;
In exile thy bosom shall still be my home,
And thine eyes make my climate wherever we roam.

To the gloom of some desert or cold rocky shore,
Where the eye of the stranger can haunt us no more,
I will fly with my Coulin, and think the rough wind
Less rude than the foes we leave frowning behind.

And I'll gaze on thy gold hair as graceful it wreathes,
And hang o'er thy soft harp, as wildly it breathes;
Nor dread that the cold-hearted Saxon will tear
One chord from that harp, or one lock from that hair.[1]

Remember the glories of Brien the brave,
  Tho' the days of the hero are o'er;
Tho' lost to Mononia and cold in the grave,
  He returns to Kinkora no more.
That star of the field, which so often hath pour'd
  Its beam on the battle, is set;
But enough of its glory remains on each sword
  To light us to victory yet.

Mononia! when Nature embellish'd the tint
Of thy fields, and thy mountains so fair,
Did she ever intend that a tyrant should print
The footstep of slavery there?
No! Freedom, whose smile we shall never resign,
Go, tell our invaders, the Danes,
That 'tis sweeter to bleed for an age at thy shrine,
Than to sleep but a moment in chains.

Forget not our wounded companions, who stood
In the day of distress by our side;
While the moss of the valley grew red with their blood,
They stirr'd not, but conquer'd and died.
That sun which now blesses our arms with his light,
Saw them fall upon Ossory's plain;—
Oh! let him not blush, when he leaves us to-night,
To find that they fell there in vain.

Fly not yet.

Fly not yet, 'tis just the hour,
When pleasure, like the midnight flower
That scorns the eye of vulgar light,
Begins to bloom for sons of night,
   And maids who love the moon.
'Twas but to bless these hours of shade
That beauty and the moon were made;
'Tis then their soft attractions glowing
Set the tides and goblets flowing.
   Oh! stay,—Oh! stay,—
Joy so seldom weaves a chain
Like this to-night, that oh, 'tis pain
   To break its links so soon.

Fly not yet, the fount that play'd
In times of old through Ammon's shade,

Though icy cold by day it ran,
Yet still, like souls of mirth, began
 To burn when night was near.
And thus, should woman's heart and looks
At noon be cold as winter brooks,
Nor kindle till the night, returning,
Brings their genial hour for burning.
 Oh! stay,—Oh! stay,—
When did morning ever break,
And find such beaming eyes awake
 As those that sparkle here?

The harp that once through Tara's halls
　The soul of music shed,
Now hangs as mute on Tara's walls,
　As if that soul were fled.—
So sleeps the pride of former days,
　So glory's thrill is o'er,
And hearts, that once beat high for praise,
　Now feel that pulse no more.

No more to chiefs and ladies bright
  The harp of Tara swells;
The chord alone, that breaks at night,
  Its tale of ruin tells.
Thus Freedom now so seldom wakes,
  The only throb she gives,
Is when some heart indignant breaks,
  To show that still she lives.

Oh! think not my spirits are always as light.

Oh! think not my spirits are always as light,
  And as free from a pang as they seem to you now;
Nor expect that the heart-beaming smile of to-night
  Will return with to-morrow to brighten my brow.

No:—life is a waste of wearisome hours,
  Which seldom the rose of enjoyment adorns;
And the heart that is soonest awake to the flowers,
  Is always the first to be touch'd by the thorns.
But send round the bowl, and be happy awhile—
  May we never meet worse, in our pilgrimage here,
Than the tear that enjoyment may gild with a smile,
  And the smile that compassion can turn to a tear.

The thread of our life would be dark, Heaven knows!
  If it were not with friendship and love intertwin'd;
And I care not how soon I may sink to repose,
  When these blessings shall cease to be dear to my mind.
But they who have lov'd the fondest, the purest,
  Too often have wept o'er the dream they believ'd;
And the heart that has slumber'd in friendship securest,
  Is happy indeed if 'twas never deceiv'd.
But send round the bowl; while a relic of truth
  Is in man or in woman, this prayer shall be mine,—
That the sunshine of love may illumine our youth,
  And the moonlight of friendship console our decline.

The meeting of the waters.

There is not in the wide world a valley so sweet
As that vale in whose bosom the bright waters meet;
Oh! the last rays of feeling and life must depart,
Ere the bloom of that valley shall fade from my heart.

Yet it *was* not that nature had shed o'er the scene
Her purest of crystal and brightest of green;
'Twas *not* her soft magic of streamlet or hill,
Oh! no—it was something more exquisite still.

'Twas that friends, the belov'd of my bosom, were near,
Who made every dear scene of enchantment more dear,
And who felt how the best charms of nature improve,
When we see them reflected from looks that we love.

As a beam o'er the face of the waters may glow.

As a beam o'er the face of the waters may glow
While the tide runs in darkness and coldness below,
So the cheek may be ting'd with a warm sunny smile,
Though the cold heart to ruin runs darkly the while.

One fatal remembrance, one sorrow that throws
Its bleak shade alike o'er our joys and our woes,
To which life nothing darker or brighter can bring
For which joy has no balm and affliction no sting—

Oh! this thought in the midst of enjoyment will stay,
Like a dead, leafless branch in the summer's bright ray;
The beams of the warm sun play round it in vain,
It may smile in his light, but it blooms not again.

D. Maclise, R.A.   F. P. Becker.

"Rich and rare were the gems she wore."

Rich and rare were the gems she wore,
And a bright gold ring on her wand she bore;
But oh! her beauty was far beyond
Her sparkling gems, or snow-white wand.

"Lady! dost thou not fear to stray,
"So lone and lovely through this bleak way?
"Are Erin's sons so good or so cold,
"As not to be tempted by woman or gold?"

"Sir Knight! I feel not the least alarm,
"No son of Erin will offer me harm:—
"For though they love woman and golden store,
"Sir Knight! they love honour and virtue more!"

D. Maclise, R.A. F. P. Becker.

On she went, and her maiden smile
In safety lighted her round the green isle;
And blest for ever is she who relied
Upon Erin's honour, and Erin's pride.

How oft has the Benshee cried.

How oft has the Benshee cried,
    How oft has death untied
    Bright links that Glory wove,
    Sweet bonds entwin'd by Love!
Peace to each manly soul that sleepeth;
Rest to each faithful eye that weepeth;
    Long may the fair and brave
    Sigh o'er the hero's grave.

We're fall'n upon gloomy days!
    Star after star decays,
    Every bright name, that shed
    Light o'er the land, is fled.
Dark falls the tear of him who mourneth
Lost joy, or hope that ne'er returneth;
    But brightly flows the tear,
    Wept o'er a hero's bier.

Quench'd are our beacon lights—
Thou, of the Hundred Fights![11]
Thou, on whose burning tongue
Truth, peace, and freedom hung![12]
Both mute,—but long as valour shineth,
Or mercy's soul at war repineth,
So long shall Erin's pride
Tell how they liv'd and died.

How dear to me the hour.

How dear to me the hour when daylight dies,
    And sunbeams melt along the silent sea,
For then sweet dreams of other days arise,
    And memory breathes her vesper sigh to thee.

And, as I watch the line of light, that plays
    Along the smooth wave tow'rd the burning west,
I long to tread that golden path of rays,
    And think 'twould lead to some bright isle of rest.

When he, who adores thee.

When he, who adores thee, has left but the name
    Of his fault and his sorrows behind,
Oh! say wilt thou weep, when they darken the fame
    Of a life that for thee was resign'd?
Yes, weep, and however my foes may condemn,
    Thy tears shall efface their decree;
For Heaven can witness, though guilty to them,
    I have been but too faithful to thee.

With thee were the dreams of my earliest love;
    Every thought of my reason was thine;
In my last humble prayer to the Spirit above,
    Thy name shall be mingled with mine.
Oh! blest are the lovers and friends who shall live
    The days of thy glory to see;
But the next dearest blessing that Heaven can give
    Is the pride of thus dying for thee.

The Legacy.

When in death I shall calmly recline,
   O bear my heart to my mistress dear;
Tell her it liv'd upon smiles and wine
   Of the brightest hue, while it linger'd here.
Bid her not shed one tear of sorrow
   To sully a heart so brilliant and light;
But balmy drops of the red grape borrow,
   To bathe the relic from morn till night.

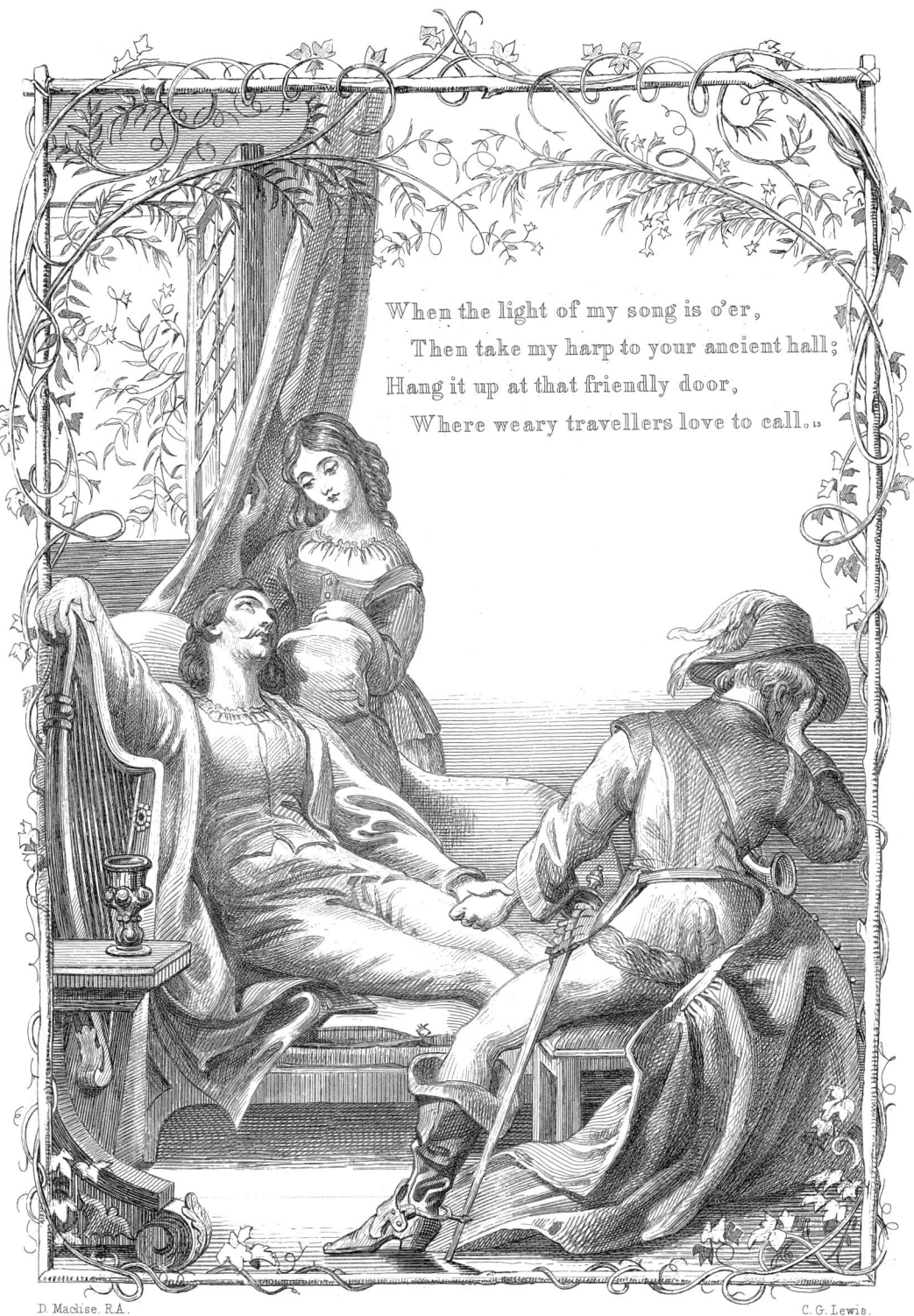

When the light of my song is o'er,
Then take my harp to your ancient hall;
Hang it up at that friendly door,
Where weary travellers love to call.

Then if some bard, who roams forsaken,
    Revive its soft note in passing along,
Oh! let one thought of its master waken
    Your warmest smile for the child of song.

Keep this cup, which is now o'erflowing,
    To grace your revel, when I'm at rest;
Never, oh! never its balm bestowing
    On lips that beauty hath seldom blest.
But when some warm devoted lover
    To her he adores shall bathe its brim,
Then, then my spirit around shall hover,
    And hallow each drop that foams for him.

Take back the virgin page.

WRITTEN ON RETURNING A BLANK BOOK.

Take back the virgin page,
    White and unwritten still;
Some hand, more calm and sage,
    The leaf must fill.
Thoughts come, as pure as light,
    Pure as even *you* require:
But, oh! each word I write
    Love turns to fire.

Yet let me keep the book:
    Oft shall my heart renew,
When on its leaves I look,
    Dear thoughts of you.
Like you, 'tis fair and bright;
    Like you, too bright and fair
To let wild passion write
    One wrong wish there.

Haply when from those eyes
    Far, far away I roam,
Should calmer thoughts arise
    Tow'rds you and home;
Fancy may trace some line,
    Worthy those eyes to meet,
Thoughts that not burn, but shine,
    Pure, calm, and sweet.

And as, o'er ocean far,
    Seamen their records keep,
Led by some hidden star
    Through the cold deep;
So may the words I write
    Tell thro' what storms I stray—
You still the unseen light,
    Guiding my way.

St. Senanus and the Lady.

St. Senanus.[14]

"Oh! haste and leave this sacred isle,
"Unholy bark, ere morning smile;
"For on thy deck, though dark it be,
"A female form I see;
"And I have sworn this sainted sod
"Shall ne'er by woman's feet be trod."

The Lady.

"Oh! Father, send not hence my bark,
"Through wintry winds and billows dark:
"I come with humble heart to share
 "Thy morn and evening prayer;
"Nor mine the feet, oh! holy Saint,
"The brightness of thy sod to taint."

The Lady's prayer Senanus spurn'd;
The winds blew fresh, the bark return'd;
But legends hint, that had the maid
 Till morning's light delay'd,
And given the saint one rosy smile,
She ne'er had left his lonely isle.

We may roam through this world.

We may roam thro' this world, like a child at a feast,
    Who but sips of a sweet, and then flies to the rest;
And, when pleasure begins to grow dull in the east,
    We may order our wings and be off to the west;
But if hearts that feel, and eyes that smile,
    Are the dearest gifts that heaven supplies,
We never need leave our own green isle,
    For sensitive hearts, and for sun-bright eyes.
Then remember, wherever your goblet is crown'd,
    Thro' this world, whether eastward or westward you roam,
When a cup to the smile of dear woman goes round,
    Oh! remember the smile that adorns her at home.

Oh! they want the wild sweet-briery fence,
　Which round the flowers of Erin dwells;
Which warns the touch, while winning the sense,
　Nor charms us least when it most repels.
Then remember, wherever your goblet is crown'd,
　Thro' this world, whether eastward or westward you roam,
When a cup to the smile of dear woman goes round,
　Oh! remember the smile that adorns her at home.

In France, when the heart of a woman sets sail,
　On the ocean of wedlock its fortune to try,
Love seldom goes far in a vessel so frail,
　But just pilots her off, and then bids her good-bye.

D. Maclise, R.A.

While the daughters of Erin keep the boy,
　Ever smiling beside his faithful oar,
Through billows of woe, and beams of joy,
　The same as he look'd when he left the shore.
Then remember, wherever your goblet is crown'd,
　Thro' this world, whether eastward or westward you roam,
When a cup to the smile of dear woman goes round,
　Oh! remember the smile that adorns her at home.

Eveleen's Bower.

　Oh! weep for the hour,
　When to Eveleen's bower
The Lord of the Valley with false vows came;
　The moon hid her light
　From the heavens that night,
And wept behind her clouds o'er the maiden's shame.

The clouds pass'd soon
From the chaste cold moon,
And heaven smil'd again with her vestal flame;
But none will see the day,
When the clouds shall pass away,
Which that dark hour left upon Eveleen's fame.

The white snow lay
On the narrow path-way,
When the Lord of the Valley crost over the moor;
And many a deep print
On the white snow's tint
Show'd the track of his footstep to Eveleen's door.

The next sun's ray
Soon melted away
Every trace on the path where the false Lord came;
But there's a light above,
Which alone can remove
That stain upon the snow of fair Eveleen's fame.

Believe me, if all those endearing Young Charms.

Believe me, if all those endearing young charms,
   Which I gaze on so fondly to-day,
Were to change by to-morrow, and fleet in my arms,
   Like fairy-gifts fading away,
Thou wouldst still be ador'd, as this moment thou art,
   Let thy loveliness fade as it will,
And around the dear ruin each wish of my heart
   Would entwine itself verdantly still.

D. Maclise, R.A.   F. P. Becker.

It is not while beauty and youth are thine own,
And thy cheeks unprofan'd by a tear,
That the fervour and faith of a soul can be known,
To which time will but make thee more dear.
No, the heart that has truly lov'd never forgets,
But as truly loves on to the close,
As the sun-flower turns on her god, when he sets,
The same look which she turn'd when he rose.

D. Maclise, R.A.

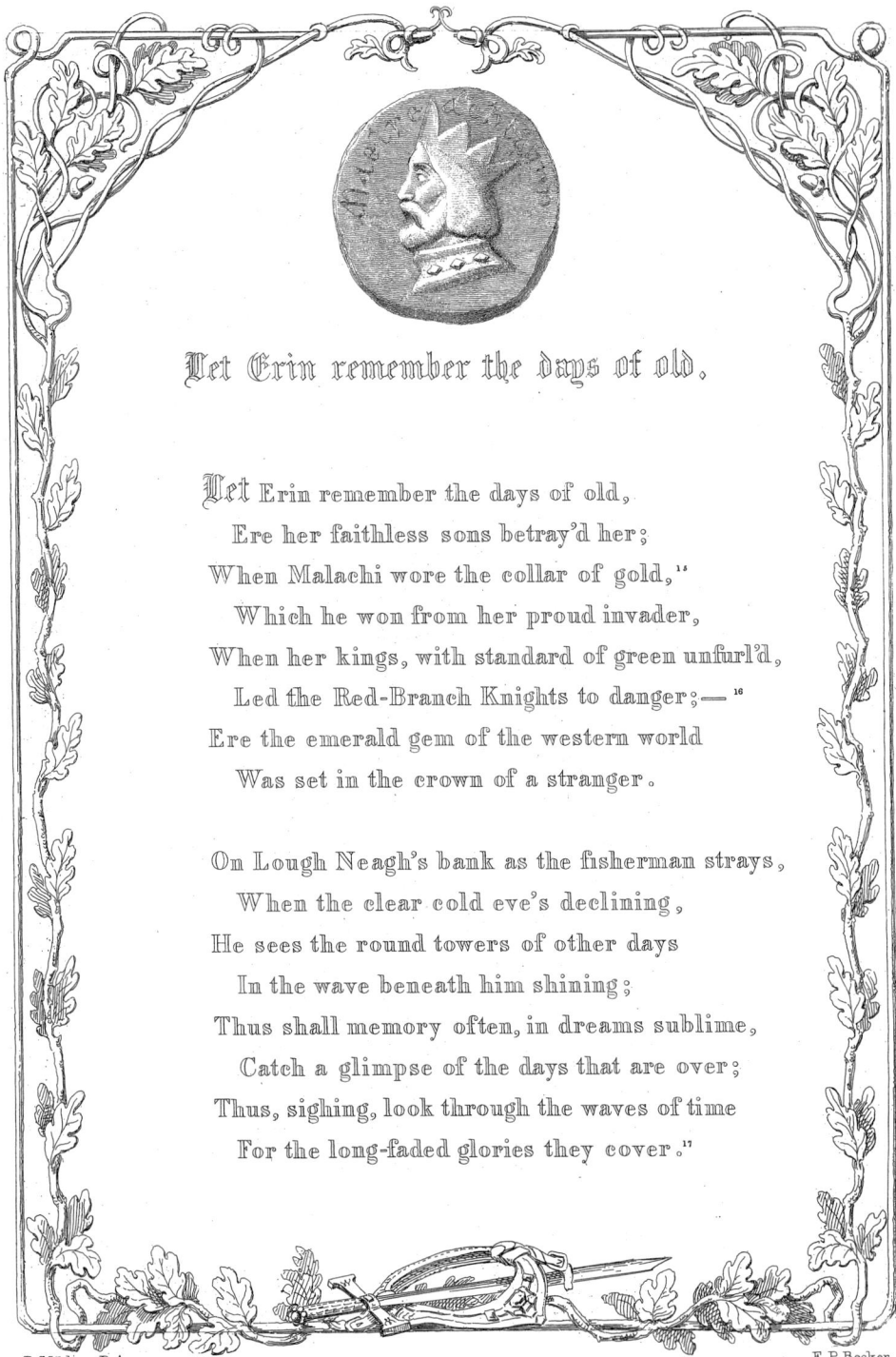

Let Erin remember the days of old.

Let Erin remember the days of old,
 Ere her faithless sons betray'd her;
When Malachi wore the collar of gold,[15]
 Which he won from her proud invader,
When her kings, with standard of green unfurl'd,
 Led the Red-Branch Knights to danger;—[16]
Ere the emerald gem of the western world
 Was set in the crown of a stranger.

On Lough Neagh's bank as the fisherman strays,
 When the clear cold eve's declining,
He sees the round towers of other days
 In the wave beneath him shining;
Thus shall memory often, in dreams sublime,
 Catch a glimpse of the days that are over;
Thus, sighing, look through the waves of time
 For the long-faded glories they cover.[17]

The Song of Fionnuala.

Silent, oh Moyle, be the roar of thy water,
    Break not, ye breezes, your chain of repose,
While, murmuring mournfully, Lir's lonely daughter
    Tells to the night-star her tale of woes.
When shall the swan, her death-note singing,
    Sleep, with wings in darkness furl'd?
When will heaven, its sweet bell ringing,
    Call my spirit from this stormy world?

Sadly, oh Moyle, to thy winter-wave weeping,
    Fate bids me languish long ages away;
Yet still in her darkness doth Erin lie sleeping,
    Still doth the pure light its dawning delay.
When will that day-star, mildly springing,
    Warm our isle with peace and love?
When will heaven, its sweet bell ringing,
    Call my spirit to the fields above?

D. Maclise, R.A.   F. P. Becker.

Come, send round the Wine.

Come, send round the wine, and leave points of belief
    To simpleton sages, and reasoning fools;
This moment's a flower too fair and brief,
    To be wither'd and stain'd by the dust of the schools.
Your glass may be purple, and mine may be blue,
    But, while they are fill'd from the same bright bowl,
The fool, who would quarrel for difference of hue,
    Deserves not the comfort they shed o'er the soul.

Shall I ask the brave soldier, who fights by my side
    In the cause of mankind, if our creeds agree?
Shall I give up the friend I have valued and tried,
    If he kneel not before the same altar with me?
From the heretic girl of my soul should I fly,
    To seek somewhere else a more orthodox kiss?
No, perish the hearts, and the laws that try
    Truth, valour, or love, by a standard like this!

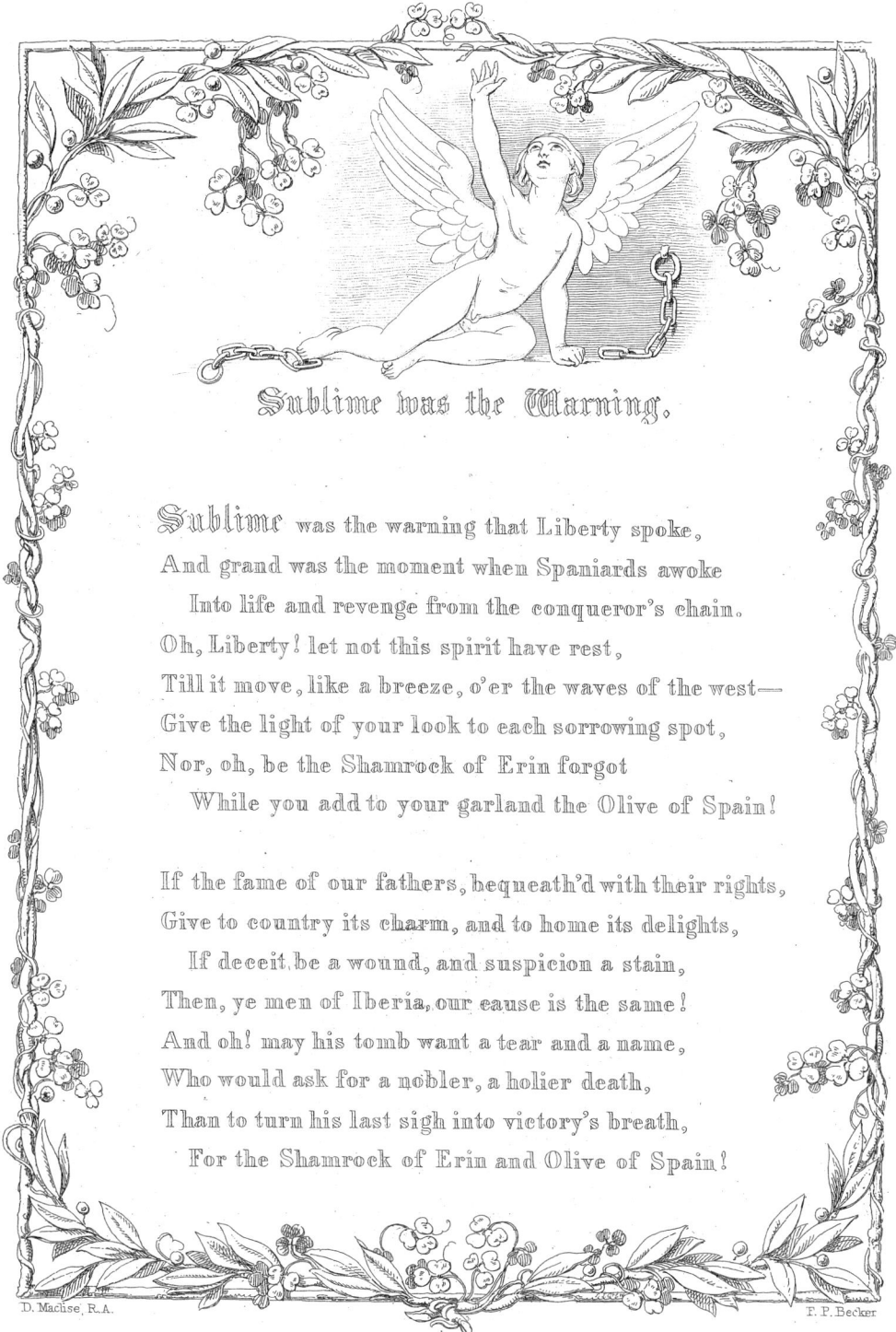

Sublime was the Warning.

Sublime was the warning that Liberty spoke,
And grand was the moment when Spaniards awoke
   Into life and revenge from the conqueror's chain.
Oh, Liberty! let not this spirit have rest,
Till it move, like a breeze, o'er the waves of the west—
Give the light of your look to each sorrowing spot,
Nor, oh, be the Shamrock of Erin forgot
   While you add to your garland the Olive of Spain!

If the fame of our fathers, bequeath'd with their rights,
Give to country its charm, and to home its delights,
   If deceit be a wound, and suspicion a stain,
Then, ye men of Iberia, our cause is the same!
And oh! may his tomb want a tear and a name,
Who would ask for a nobler, a holier death,
Than to turn his last sigh into victory's breath,
   For the Shamrock of Erin and Olive of Spain!

D. Maclise, R.A.   F. P. Becker

Ye Blakes and O'Donnels, whose fathers resign'd
The green hills of their youth, among strangers to find
    That repose which, at home, they had sigh'd for in vain,
Join, join in our hope that the flame, which you light,
May be felt yet in Erin, as calm, and as bright,
And forgive even Albion while blushing she draws,
Like a truant, her sword, in the long-slighted cause
    Of the Shamrock of Erin and Olive of Spain!

God prosper the cause!—oh, it cannot but thrive,
While the pulse of one patriot heart is alive,
    Its devotion to feel, and its rights to maintain;
Then, how sainted by sorrow, its martyrs will die!
The finger of Glory shall point where they lie;
While, far from the footstep of coward or slave,
The young spirit of Freedom shall shelter their grave
    Beneath Shamrocks of Erin and Olives of Spain!

Erin, oh Erin.

Like the bright lamp, that shone in Kildare's holy fane,[19]
    And burn'd thro' long ages of darkness and storm,
Is the heart that sorrows have frown'd on in vain,
    Whose spirit outlives them, unfading and warm.
Erin, oh Erin, thus bright thro' the tears
Of a long night of bondage, thy spirit appears.

The nations have fallen, and thou still art young,
    Thy sun is but rising, when others are set;
And tho' slavery's cloud o'er thy morning hath hung
    The full noon of freedom shall beam round thee yet.

Erin, oh Erin, tho' long in the shade,
Thy star will shine out when the proudest shall fade.

Unchill'd by the rain, and unwak'd by the wind,
   The lily lies sleeping thro' winter's cold hour,
Till Spring's light touch her fetters unbind,
   And daylight and liberty bless the young flower."[20]
Thus Erin, oh Erin, *thy* winter is past,
And the hope that liv'd thro' it shall blossom at last.

Oh! blame not the bard, if he fly to the bowers,
 Where Pleasure lies, carelessly smiling at Fame;
He was born for much more, and in happier hours
 His soul might have burn'd with a holier flame.
The string, that now languishes loose o'er the lyre,
 Might have bent a proud bow to the warrior's dart;
And the lip, which now breathes but the song of desire,
 Might have pour'd the full tide of a patriot's heart.

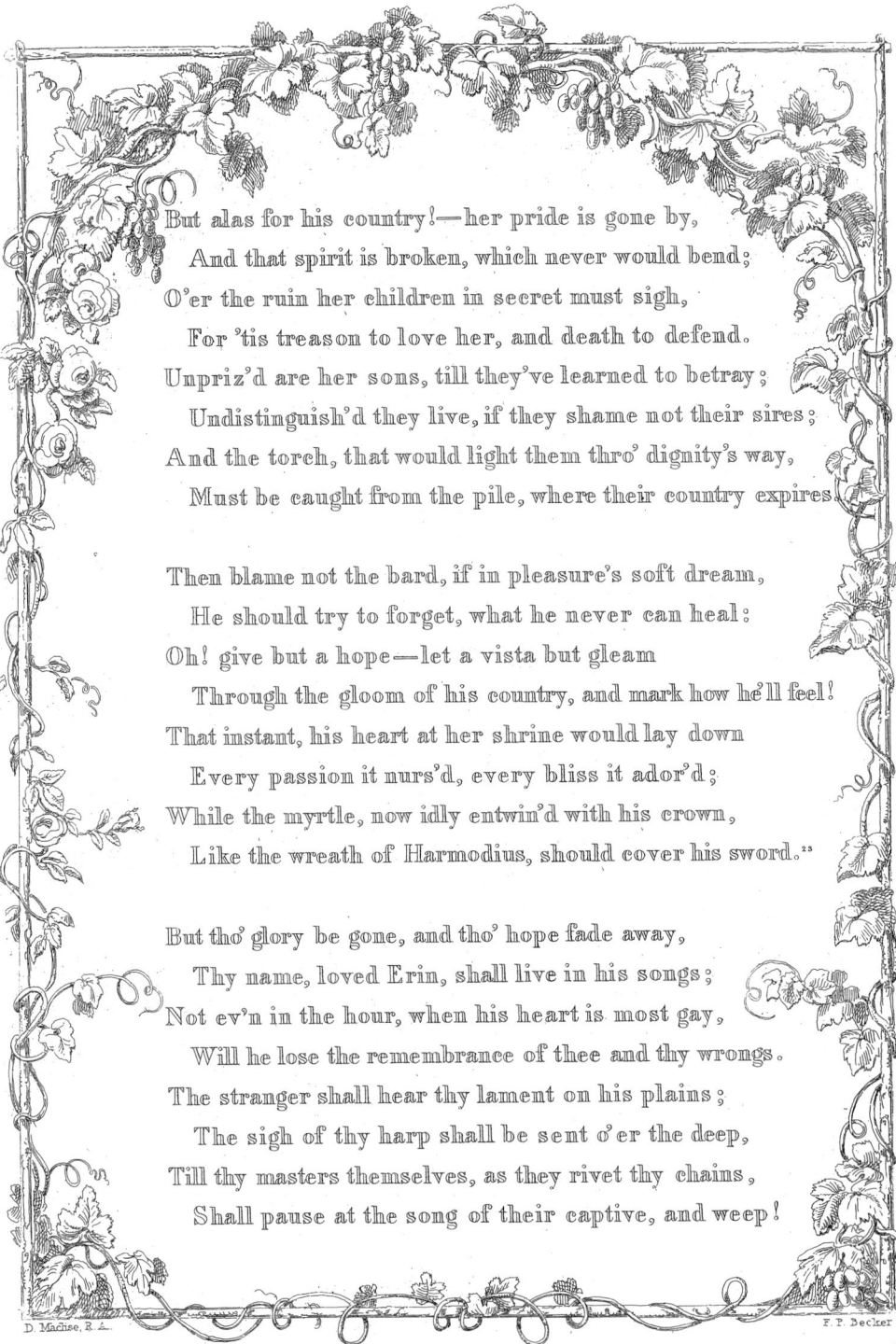

But alas for his country!—her pride is gone by,
    And that spirit is broken, which never would bend;
O'er the ruin her children in secret must sigh,
    For 'tis treason to love her, and death to defend.
Unpriz'd are her sons, till they've learned to betray;
    Undistinguish'd they live, if they shame not their sires;
And the torch, that would light them thro' dignity's way,
    Must be caught from the pile, where their country expires.

Then blame not the bard, if in pleasure's soft dream,
    He should try to forget, what he never can heal:
Oh! give but a hope—let a vista but gleam
    Through the gloom of his country, and mark how he'll feel!
That instant, his heart at her shrine would lay down
    Every passion it nurs'd, every bliss it ador'd;
While the myrtle, now idly entwin'd with his crown,
    Like the wreath of Harmodius, should cover his sword.[23]

But tho' glory be gone, and tho' hope fade away,
    Thy name, loved Erin, shall live in his songs;
Not ev'n in the hour, when his heart is most gay,
    Will he lose the remembrance of thee and thy wrongs.
The stranger shall hear thy lament on his plains;
    The sigh of thy harp shall be sent o'er the deep,
Till thy masters themselves, as they rivet thy chains,
    Shall pause at the song of their captive, and weep!

Drink to her.

Drink to her, who long
    Hath wak'd the poet's sigh,
The girl, who gave to song
    What gold could never buy.
Oh! woman's heart was made
    For minstrel hands alone;
By other fingers play'd,
    It yields not half the tone.
Then here's to her, who long
    Hath wak'd the poet's sigh,
The girl who gave to song
    What gold could never buy.

At Beauty's door of glass,
When Wealth and Wit once stood,
They ask'd her, "which might pass?"
She answer'd, "he, who could."

With golden key Wealth thought
  To pass—but 'twould not do:
While Wit a diamond brought,
  Which cut his bright way through.
So here's to her, who long
  Hath wak'd the poet's sigh,
The girl, who gave to song
  What gold could never buy.

The love that seeks a home
  Where wealth or grandeur shines,
Is like the gloomy gnome,
  That dwells in dark gold mines.
But oh! the poet's love
  Can boast a brighter sphere;
Its native home's above,
  Tho' woman keeps it here.
Then drink to her, who long
  Hath wak'd the poet's sigh,
The girl, who gave to song
  What gold could never buy.

While gazing on the Moon's light.

While gazing on the moon's light,
    A moment from her smile I turn'd,
To look at orbs, that, more bright,
    In lone and distant glory burn'd.
        But *too* far
        Each proud star,
For me to feel its warming flame;
        Much more dear
        That mild sphere,
Which near our planet smiling came;[24]
Thus, Mary, be but thou my own;
    While brighter eyes unheeded play,
I'll love those moonlight looks alone,
    That bless my home and guide my way.

The day had sunk in dim showers,
    But midnight now, with lustre meet,
Illumin'd all the pale flowers,
    Like hope upon a mourner's cheek.
        I said (while
        The moon's smile
Play'd o'er a stream, in dimpling bliss,)
      "The moon looks
      "On many brooks,
"The brook can see no moon but this;"
And thus, I thought, our fortunes run,
    For many a lover looks to thee,
While oh! I feel there is but *one*,
    One Mary in the world for me.

Ill Omens.

When daylight was yet sleeping under the billow,
   And stars in the heavens still lingering shone,
Young Kitty, all blushing, rose up from her pillow,
   The last time she e'er was to press it alone.
For the youth whom she treasured her heart and her soul in,
   Had promised to link the last tie before noon;
And when once the young heart of a maiden is stolen
   The maiden herself will steal after it soon.

As she look'd in the glass, which a woman ne'er misses,
   Nor ever wants time for a sly glance or two,
A butterfly,[26] fresh from the night-flower's kisses,
   Flew over the mirror, and shaded her view.
Enrag'd with the insect for hiding her graces,
   She brush'd him—he fell, alas; never to rise:
"Ah! such," said the girl, "is the pride of our faces,
   "For which the soul's innocence too often dies."

While she stole thro' the garden, where hearts-ease was growing,
　She cull'd some, and kiss'd off its night-fallen dew;
And a rose, further on, look'd so tempting and glowing,
　That, spite of her haste, she must gather it too:
But while o'er the roses too carelessly leaning,
　Her zone flew in two, and the hearts-ease was lost:
"Ah! this means," said the girl (and she sigh'd at its meaning),
　"That love is scarce worth the repose it will cost!"

D. Maclise, R.A.　　　　　　　　　　　　　　　　　　　　H. Robinson.

Before the Battle.

By the hope within us springing,
   Herald of to-morrow's strife;
By that sun, whose light is bringing
   Chains or freedom, death or life—
   Oh! remember life can be
No charm for him, who lives not free!
   Like the day-star in the wave,
   Sinks a hero in his grave,
Midst the dew-fall of a nation's tears.

Happy is he o'er whose decline
   The smiles of home may soothing shine
And light him down the steep of years:—
   But oh, how blest they sink to rest,
   Who close their eyes on victory's breast!

O'er his watch-fire's fading embers
    Now the foeman's cheek turns white,
When his heart that field remembers,
    Where we tamed his tyrant might.
Never let him bind again
A chain, like that we broke from then.
    Hark! the horn of combat calls—
    Ere the golden evening falls,
May we pledge that horn in triumph round! [27]

Many a heart that now beats high,
In slumber cold at night shall lie,
Nor waken even at victory's sound:—
    But oh, how blest that hero's sleep,
    O'er whom a wond'ring world shall weep!

After the Battle.

Night clos'd around the conqueror's way,
    And lightnings show'd the distant hill,
Where those who lost that dreadful day,
    Stood few and faint, but fearless still.
The soldier's hope, the patriot's zeal,
    For ever dimm'd, for ever crost—
Oh! who shall say what heroes feel,
    When all but life and honour's lost?

The last sad hour of freedom's dream,
    And valour's task, moved slowly by,
While mute they watch'd, till morning's beam
    Should rise and give them light to die.
There's yet a world, where souls are free,
    Where tyrants taint not nature's bliss;—
If death that world's bright opening be,
    Oh! who would live a slave in this?

Oh! had we some bright little Isle of our own.

Oh! had we some bright little isle of our own,
In a blue summer ocean, far off and alone,
Where a leaf never dies in the still blooming bowers,
And the bee banquets on through a whole year of flowers;
    Where the sun loves to pause
      With so fond a delay,
    That the night only draws
      A thin veil o'er the day;
Where simply to feel that we breathe, that we live,
Is worth the best joy that life elsewhere can give.

There, with souls ever ardent and pure as the clime,
We should love, as they lov'd in the first golden time;
The glow of the sunshine, the balm of the air,
Would steal to our hearts, and make all summer there.
    With affection as free
      From decline as the bowers,
    And, with hope, like the bee,
      Living always on flowers,
Our life should resemble a long day of light,
And our death come on, holy and calm as the night.

The Irish Peasant to his Mistress.

Through grief and through danger thy smile hath cheer'd my way,
Till hope seem'd to bud from each thorn that round me lay;
The darker our fortune, the brighter our pure love burn'd,
Till shame into glory, till fear into zeal was turn'd;
Yes, slave as I was, in thy arms my spirit felt free,
And bless'd even the sorrows that made me more dear to thee.

Thy rival was honour'd, while thou wert wrong'd
 and scorn'd,
Thy crown was of briers, while gold her brows
 adorn'd;
She woo'd me to temples, while thou lay'st hid in
 caves,
Her friends were all masters, while thine, alas! were
 slaves;
Yet cold in the earth, at thy feet, I would rather be,
Than wed what I lov'd not, or turn one thought from
 thee.

They slander thee sorely, who say thy vows are
 frail—
Hadst thou been a false one, thy cheek had look'd
 less pale.
They say, too, so long thou hast worn those lingering
 chains,
That deep in thy heart they have printed their servile
 stains—
Oh! foul is the slander,—no chain could that soul
 subdue—
Where shineth *thy* spirit, there liberty shineth too! [29]

The origin of the Harp.

'Tis believ'd that this Harp, which I wake now for thee,
Was a Siren of old, who sung under the sea;
And who often, at eve, thro' the bright waters rov'd,
To meet, on the green shore, a youth whom she lov'd.

But she lov'd him in vain, for he left her to weep,
And in tears, all the night her gold tresses to steep;
Till heav'n look'd with pity on true-love so warm,
And chang'd to this soft Harp the sea-maiden's form.

Still her bosom rose fair—still her cheeks smil'd the same—
While her sea-beauties gracefully form'd the light frame;
And her hair, as, let loose, o'er her white arm it fell,
Was chang'd to bright chords utt'ring melody's spell.

Hence it came, that this soft Harp so long hath been known
To mingle love's language with sorrow's sad tone;
Till *thou* didst divide them, and teach the fond lay
To speak love when I'm near thee, and grief when away.

Weep on, Weep on.

Weep on, weep on, your hour is past;
   Your dreams of pride are o'er;
The fatal chain is round you cast,
   And you are men no more.
In vain the hero's heart hath bled;
   The sage's tongue hath warn'd in vain;—
Oh, Freedom! once thy flame hath fled,
   It never lights again.

Weep on—perhaps in after days,
    They'll learn to love your name;
When many a deed may wake in praise
    That long hath slept in blame.
And when they tread the ruin'd isle,
    Where rest, at length, the lord and slave,
They'll wondering ask, how hands so vile
    Could conquer hearts so brave?

"'Twas fate," they'll say, "a wayward fate
" "Your web of discord wove;
"And while your tyrants join'd in hate,
" You never join'd in love.
"But hearts fell off, that ought to twine,
" And man profan'd what God had given;
"Till some were heard to curse the shrine,
" Where others knelt to heaven!"

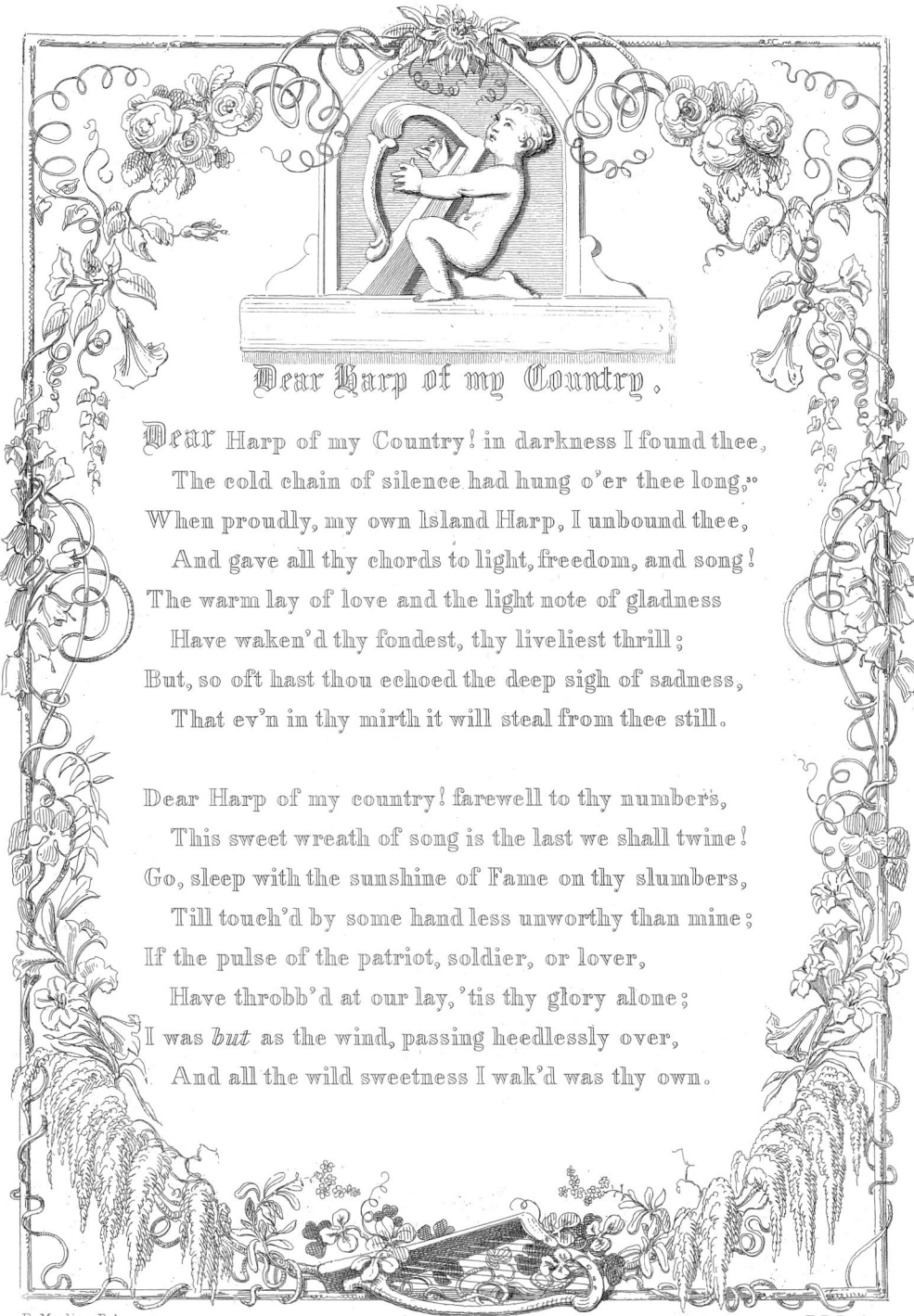

Dear Harp of my Country.

Dear Harp of my Country! in darkness I found thee,
    The cold chain of silence had hung o'er thee long,
When proudly, my own Island Harp, I unbound thee,
    And gave all thy chords to light, freedom, and song!
The warm lay of love and the light note of gladness
    Have waken'd thy fondest, thy liveliest thrill;
But, so oft hast thou echoed the deep sigh of sadness,
    That ev'n in thy mirth it will steal from thee still.

Dear Harp of my country! farewell to thy numbers,
    This sweet wreath of song is the last we shall twine!
Go, sleep with the sunshine of Fame on thy slumbers,
    Till touch'd by some hand less unworthy than mine;
If the pulse of the patriot, soldier, or lover,
    Have throbb'd at our lay, 'tis thy glory alone;
I was *but* as the wind, passing heedlessly over,
    And all the wild sweetness I wak'd was thy own.

D. Maclise, R.A.   F. P. Becker.

Love's Young Dream.

Oh! the days are gone, when Beauty bright
    My heart's chain wove;
When my dream of life, from morn till night,
    Was love, still love.
    New hope may bloom,
    And days may come,
Of milder calmer beam,
But there's nothing half so sweet in life
  As love's young dream:
No, there's nothing half so sweet in life
  As love's young dream.

Tho' the bard to purer fame may soar,
    When wild youth's past;
Tho' he win the wise, who frown'd before,
    To smile at last;
    He'll never meet
    A joy so sweet,
In all his noon of fame,
As when first he sung to woman's ear
  His soul-felt flame,
And, at every close, she blush'd to hear
  The one lov'd name.

No,—that hallow'd form is ne'er forgot
Which first love trac'd;
Still it lingering haunts the greenest spot
On memory's waste.
'Twas odour fled
As soon as shed;
'Twas morning's winged dream;
'Twas a light, that ne'er can shine again
On life's dull stream:
Oh! 'twas light that ne'er can shine again
On life's dull stream.

The Prince's Day.

Tho' dark are our sorrows, to-day we'll forget them,
    And smile through our tears, like a sunbeam in showers:
There never were hearts, if our rulers would let them,
    More form'd to be grateful and blest than ours.
          But just when the chain
          Has ceas'd to pain,
    And hope has enwreath'd it round with flowers,
          There comes a new link
          Our spirits to sink—
Oh! the joy that we taste, like the light of the poles,
    Is a flash amid darkness, too brilliant to stay;
But, though 'twere the last little spark in our souls,
    We must light it up now, on our Prince's Day.

Contempt on the minion, who calls you disloyal!
    Tho' fierce to your foe, to your friends you are true;
And the tribute most high to a head that is royal,
    Is love from a heart that loves liberty too.

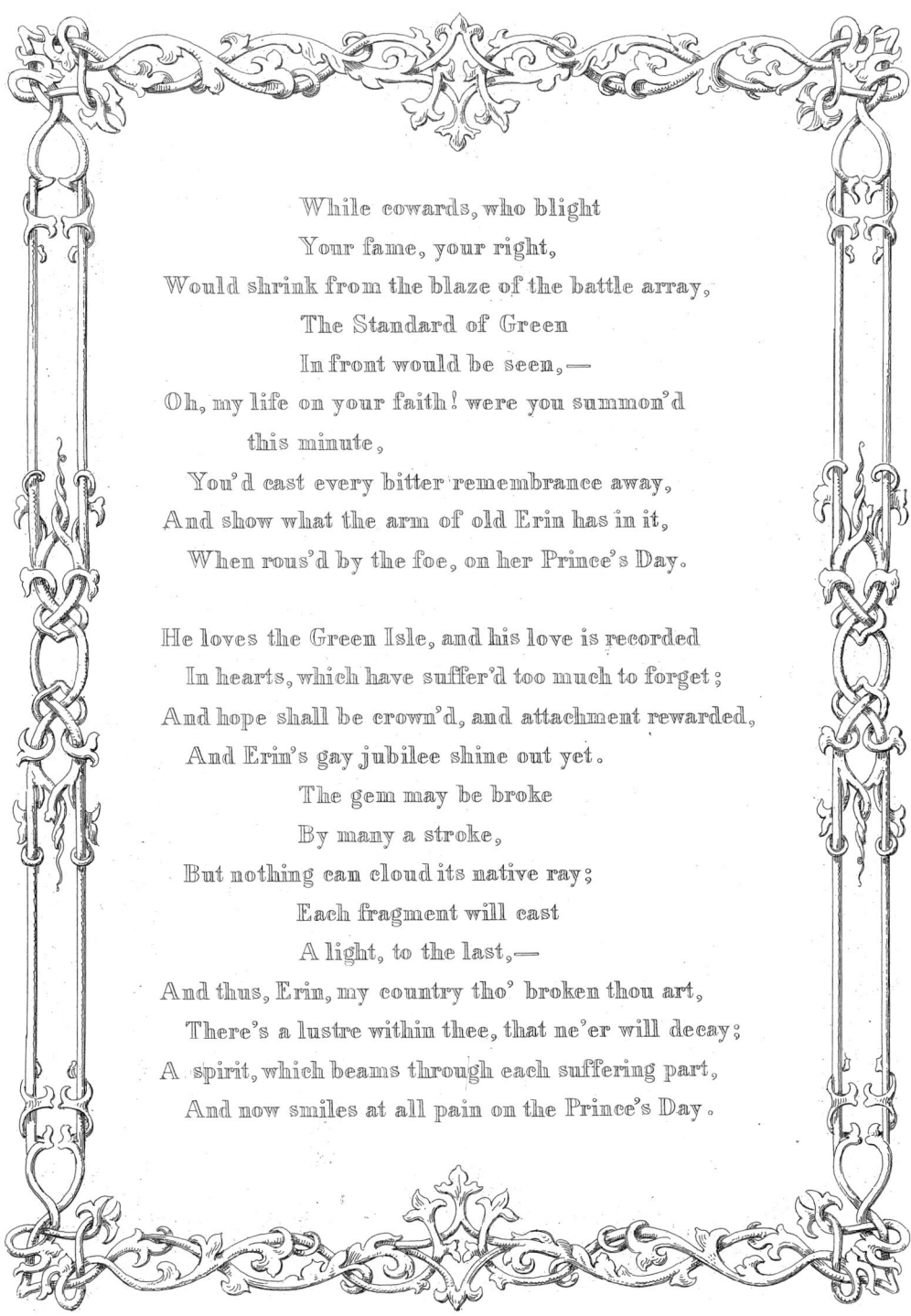

   While cowards, who blight
    Your fame, your right,
Would shrink from the blaze of the battle array,
    The Standard of Green
    In front would be seen,—
  Oh, my life on your faith! were you summon'd
     this minute,
  You'd cast every bitter remembrance away,
And show what the arm of old Erin has in it,
  When rous'd by the foe, on her Prince's Day.

He loves the Green Isle, and his love is recorded
  In hearts, which have suffer'd too much to forget;
And hope shall be crown'd, and attachment rewarded,
  And Erin's gay jubilee shine out yet.
    The gem may be broke
    By many a stroke,
  But nothing can cloud its native ray;
    Each fragment will cast
    A light, to the last,—
And thus, Erin, my country tho' broken thou art,
  There's a lustre within thee, that ne'er will decay;
A spirit, which beams through each suffering part,
  And now smiles at all pain on the Prince's Day.

Lesbia hath a beaming eye,
  But no one knows for whom it beameth;
Right and left its arrows fly,
  But what they aim at no one dreameth.
Sweeter 'tis to gaze upon
  My Nora's lid that seldom rises;
Few its looks, but every one,
  Like unexpected light, surprises!
    Oh, my Nora Creina, dear,
  My gentle, bashful Nora Creina,
    Beauty lies
    In many eyes,
  But Love in yours, my Nora Creina.

Lesbia wears a robe of gold,
    But all so close the nymph hath lac'd it,
Not a charm of beauty's mould
    Presumes to stay where nature plac'd it.
Oh! my Nora's gown for me,
    That floats as wild as mountain breezes,
Leaving every beauty free
    To sink or swell as Heaven pleases.
      Yes, my Nora Creina, dear,
My simple, graceful Nora Creina,
        Nature's dress
        Is loveliness—
The dress *you* wear, my Nora Creina.

Lesbia hath a wit refin'd,
    But, when its points are gleaming round us,
Who can tell if they're design'd
    To dazzle merely, or to wound us?
Pillow'd on my Nora's heart,
    In safer slumber Love reposes—
Bed of peace! whose roughest part
    Is but the crumpling of the roses.

By that Lake, whose gloomy shore.

By that Lake, whose gloomy shore
Sky-lark never warbles o'er,
Where the cliff hangs high and steep,
Young Saint Kevin stole to sleep.
"Here, at least," he calmly said,
"Woman ne'er shall find my bed."
Ah! the good Saint little knew
What that wily sex can do.

'Twas from Kathleen's eyes he flew,—
Eyes of most unholy blue!
She had lov'd him well and long,
Wish'd him hers, nor thought it wrong.
Wheresoe'er the Saint would fly,
Still he heard her light foot nigh;
East or west, where'er he turn'd,
Still her eyes before him burn'd.

On the bold cliff's bosom cast,
Tranquil now he sleeps at last;
Dreams of heav'n, nor thinks that e'er
Woman's smile can haunt him there.
But nor earth nor heaven is free
From her power, if fond she be:
Even now, while calm he sleeps,
Kathleen o'er him leans and weeps.

Fearless she had track'd his feet
To this rocky, wild retreat;
And when morning met his view,
Her mild glances met it too.
Ah, your Saints have cruel hearts!
Sternly from his bed he starts,
And with rude, repulsive shock,
Hurls her from the beetling rock.

Glendalough, thy gloomy wave
Soon was gentle Kathleen's grave!
Soon the saint (yet ah! too late,)
Felt her love, and mourn'd her fate.
When he said, "Heav'n rest her soul!"
Round the Lake light music stole;
And her ghost was seen to glide,
Smiling o'er the fatal tide.

It is not the tear at this moment shed.[34]

It is not the tear at this moment shed,
    When the cold turf has just been laid o'er him,
That can tell how belov'd was the friend that's fled,
    Or how deep in our hearts we deplore him.
'Tis the tear, thro' many a long day wept,
    'Tis life's whole path o'ershaded;
'Tis the one remembrance, fondly kept,
    When all lighter griefs have faded.

Thus his memory, like some holy light,
    Kept alive in our hearts, will improve them,
For worth shall look fairer, and truth more bright,
    When we think how he liv'd but to love them.
And, as fresher flowers the sod perfume
    Where buried saints are lying,
So our hearts shall borrow a sweet'ning bloom
    From the image he left there in dying!

I saw thy Form in Youthful Prime.

I saw thy form in youthful prime,
   Nor thought that pale decay
Would steal before the steps of Time,
   And waste its bloom away, Mary!
Yet still thy features wore that light,
   Which fleets not with the breath;
And life ne'er look'd more truly bright
   Than in thy smile of death, Mary!

As streams that run o'er golden mines,
   Yet humbly, calmly glide,
Nor seem to know the wealth that shines
   Within their gentle tide, Mary!
So veil'd beneath the simplest guise,
   Thy radiant genius shone,
And that, which charm'd all other eyes,
   Seem'd worthless in thine own, Mary!

D. Maclise, R.A.   F. P. Becker.

If souls could always dwell above,
 Thou ne'er hadst left that sphere;
Or could we keep the souls we love,
 We ne'er had lost thee here, Mary!
Though many a gifted mind we meet,
 Though fairest forms we see,
To live with them is far less sweet,
 Than to remember thee, Mary!"

Love and the Novice.

"Here we dwell, in holiest bowers,
 "Where angels of light o'er our orisons bend;
"Where sighs of devotion and breathings of flowers
 "To heaven in mingled odour ascend.
"Do not disturb our calm, oh Love!
 "So like is thy form to the cherubs above,
"It well might deceive such hearts as ours."

Love stood near the Novice and listen'd,
    And Love is no novice in taking a hint;
His laughing blue eyes soon with piety glisten'd;
    His rosy wing turn'd to heaven's own tint.
        "Who would have thought," the urchin cries,
          "That Love could so well, so gravely disguise
"His wandering wings, and wounding eyes?"

Love now warms thee, waking and sleeping,
    Young Novice, to him all thy orisons rise.
He tinges the heavenly fount with his weeping,
    He brightens the censer's flame with his sighs.
        Love is the Saint enshrin'd in thy breast,
        And angels themselves would admit such a guest,
If he came to them cloth'd in Piety's vest.

D. Maclise, R.A.   F. P. Becker.

Avenging and Bright.

Avenging and bright fall the swift sword of Erin[36]
   On him who the brave sons of Usna betray'd!—
For ev'ry fond eye he hath waken'd a tear in,
   A drop from his heart-wounds shall weep o'er her blade.

By the red cloud that hung over Conor's dark dwelling,[37]
   When Ulad's[38] three champions lay sleeping in gore—
By the billows of war, which so often, high swelling,
   Have wafted these heroes to victory's shore—

We swear to revenge them!—no joy shall be tasted,
   The harp shall be silent, the maiden unwed,
Our halls shall be mute and our fields shall lie wasted,
   Till vengeance is wreak'd on the murderer's head.

Yes, monarch! tho' sweet are our home recollections,
   Though sweet are the tears that from tenderness fall;
Though sweet are our friendships, our hopes, our affections,
   Revenge on a tyrant is sweetest of all!

D. Maclise, R.A.   F. P. Becker.

What the bee is to the floweret.

He.— What the bee is to the floweret,
    When he looks for honey-dew,
  Through the leaves that close embower it,
    That, my love, I'll be to you.

She.— What the bank, with verdure glowing,
    Is to waves that wander near,
  Whispering kisses, while they're going,
    That I'll be to you, my dear.

She.— But they say, the bee's a rover,
    Who will fly, when sweets are gone;
  And, when once the kiss is over,
    Faithless brooks will wander on.

He.— Nay, if flowers *will* lose their looks,
    If sunny banks *will* wear away,
  'Tis but right, that bees and brooks
    Should sip and kiss them, while they may.

She is far from the land.

She is far from the land where her young hero sleeps,
    And lovers are round her, sighing:
But coldly she turns from their gaze, and weeps,
    For her heart in his grave is lying.

She sings the wild song of her dear native plains,
    Every note which he lov'd awaking;—
Ah! little they think who delight in her strains,
    How the heart of the Minstrel is breaking.

He had liv'd for his love, for his country he died,
    They were all that to life had entwin'd him;
Nor soon shall the tears of his country be dried,
    Nor long will his love stay behind him.

Oh! make her a grave where the sunbeams rest,
    When they promise a glorious morrow;
They'll shine o'er her sleep like a smile from the West,
    From her own loved island of sorrow.

Nay, tell me not, Dear.

Nay, tell me not, dear, that the goblet drowns
One charm of feeling, one fond regret;
Believe me, a few of thy angry frowns
Are all I've sunk in its bright wave yet.

Ne'er hath a beam
  Been lost in the stream
That ever was shed from thy form or soul;
  The spell of those eyes,
  The balm of thy sighs,
Still float on the surface, and hallow my bowl.
Then fancy not, dearest, that wine can steal
  One blissful dream of the heart from me;
Like founts that awaken the pilgrim's zeal,
  The bowl but brightens my love for thee.

They tell us that Love in his fairy bower
  Had two blush-roses, of birth divine;
He sprinkled the one with a rainbow's shower,
  But bath'd the other with mantling wine.
  Soon did the buds
  That drank of the floods
Distill'd by the rainbow, decline and fade;
  While those which the tide
  Of ruby had dy'd
All blush'd into beauty, like thee, sweet maid!
Then fancy not, dearest, that wine can steal
  One blissful dream of the heart from me;
Like founts, that awaken the pilgrim's zeal,
  The bowl but brightens my love for thee.

At the mid hour of Night.

At the mid hour of night, when stars are weeping, I fly
To the lone vale we lov'd, when life shone warm in thine eye;
   And I think oft, if spirits can steal from the regions
      of air,
   To revisit past scenes of delight, thou wilt come
      to me there,
And tell me our love is remember'd, even in the sky.

Then I sing the wild song 'twas once such pleasure to hear!
When our voices commingling breath'd, like one, on the ear;
   And, as Echo far off through the vale my sad orison
      rolls,
   I think, oh my love! 'tis thy voice from the King-
      dom of Souls,"
Faintly answering still the notes that once were so dear.

The young May moon is beaming, love,
The glow-worm's lamp is gleaming, love,
    How sweet to rove
       Through Morna's grove,[40]
When the drowsy world is dreaming, love!
Then awake!—the heavens look bright, my dear;
'Tis never too late for delight, my dear;
    And the best of all ways
       To lengthen our days,
Is to steal a few hours from the night, my dear!

D. Maclise, R.A.   F. P. Becker.

This life is all chequer'd with pleasures and woes.

This life is all chequer'd with pleasures and woes,
  That chase one another like waves of the deep,—
Each brightly or darkly, as onward it flows,
  Reflecting our eyes, as they sparkle or weep.
So closely our whims on our miseries tread,
  That the laugh is awak'd ere the tear can be dried;
And, as fast as the rain-drop of Pity is shed,
  The goose-plumage of Folly can turn it aside.
But pledge me the cup—if existence would cloy,
  With hearts ever happy, and heads ever wise,
Be ours the light Sorrow, half-sister to Joy,
  And the light, brilliant Folly that flashes and dies.

When Hylas was sent with his urn to the fount,
  Thro' fields full of light, and with heart full of play,

D. Maclise, R.A.   F. P. Becker.

Light rambled the boy, over meadow and mount,
    And neglected his task for the flowers on the way."⁴¹
Thus many, like me, who in youth should have tasted
    The fountain that runs by Philosophy's shrine,
Their time with the flowers on the margin have wasted,
    And left their light urns all as empty as mine.
But pledge me the goblet;—while Idleness weaves
    These flowerets together, should Wisdom but see
One bright drop or two that has fall'n on the leaves
    From her fountain divine, 'tis sufficient for me.

D. Maclise, R.A.   F. P. Becker.

Oh the Shamrock.

Through Erin's Isle,
To sport awhile,
As Love and Valour wander'd,
With Wit, the sprite,
Whose quiver bright
A thousand arrows squander'd.
Where'er they pass,
A triple grass[42]
Shoots up, with dew-drops streaming,
As softly green
As emeralds seen
Thro' purest crystal gleaming.
Oh the Shamrock, the green, immortal Shamrock!
Chosen leaf
Of Bard and Chief,
Old Erin's native Shamrock!

D. Maclise, R.A.   F. P. Becker.

Says Valour, "See,
"They spring for me,
"Those leafy gems of morning!"—
Says Love, "No, no,
"For *me* they grow,
"My fragrant path adorning."

But Wit perceives
The triple leaves,
And cries, "Oh! do not sever
"A type, that blends
"Three godlike friends,
"Love, Valour, Wit, for ever!"

Oh the Shamrock, the green, immortal Shamrock!
Chosen leaf
Of Bard and Chief,
Old Erin's native Shamrock!

So firmly fond
May last the bond,
They wove that morn together,
And ne'er may fall
One drop of gall
On Wit's celestial feather.
May Love, as twine
His flowers divine,
Of thorny falsehood weed 'em;
May Valour ne'er
His standard rear
Against the cause of Freedom!
Oh the Shamrock, the green, immortal Shamrock!
Chosen leaf
Of Bard and Chief,
Old Erin's native Shamrock!

D. Maclise, R.A.   F. P. Becker.

The Song of O'Ruark,

PRINCE OF BREFFNI [43]

The valley lay smiling before me,
   Where lately I left her behind;
Yet I trembled, and something hung o'er me,
   That saddened the joy of my mind.
I look'd for the lamp which, she told me,
   Should shine, when her Pilgrim return'd;
But, though darkness began to infold me,
   No lamp from the battlements burn'd!

I flew to her chamber—'twas lonely,
   As if the lov'd tenant lay dead;—
Ah, would it were death, and death only!
   But no, the young false one had fled.
And there hung the lute that could soften
   My very worst pains into bliss;
While the hand, that had wak'd it so often,
   Now throbb'd to a proud rival's kiss.

D. Maclise, R.A.   F. P. Becker.

There *was* a time, falsest of women,
    When Breffni's good sword would have sought
That man, thro' a million of foemen,
    Who dar'd but to wrong thee *in thought!*
While now—oh degenerate daughter
    Of Erin, how fall'n is thy fame!
And thro' ages of bondage and slaughter,
    Our country shall bleed for thy shame.

Already, the curse is upon her,
    And strangers her valleys profane;
They come to divide, to dishonour,
    And tyrants they long will remain.
But onward!—the green banner rearing,
    Go, flesh every sword to the hilt;
On *our* side is Virtue and Erin,
    On *theirs* is the Saxon and Guilt.

"You remember Ellen, our hamlet's pride,
How meekly she blessed her humble lot,
When the stranger, William, had made her his bride,
And love was the light of their lowly cot.
Together they toil'd through winds and rains,
Till William, at length, in sadness said,
"We must seek our fortune on other plains;"—
Then, sighing, she left her lowly shed.

They roam'd a long and a weary way,
    Nor much was the maiden's heart at ease,
When now, at close of one stormy day,
    They see a proud castle among the trees.
"To-night," said the youth, "we'll shelter there;
    "The wind blows cold, the hour is late:"
So he blew the horn with a chieftain's air,
    And the Porter bow'd, as they pass'd the gate.

"Now, welcome, Lady," exclaim'd the youth,—
    "This castle is thine, and these dark woods all!"
She believ'd him crazed, but his words were truth,
    For Ellen is Lady of Rosna Hall!
And dearly the Lord of Rosna loves
    What William the stranger woo'd and wed;
And the light of bliss, in these lordly groves,
    Shines pure as it did in the lowly shed.

D. Maclise, R.A.   F. P. Becker.

'Tis the last rose of summer.

'Tis the last rose of summer
  Left blooming alone;
All her lovely companions
  Are faded and gone;
No flower of her kindred,
  No rose-bud is nigh,
To reflect back her blushes,
  Or give sigh for sigh.

I'll not leave thee, thou lone one!
  To pine on the stem;
Since the lovely are sleeping,
  Go, sleep thou with them.
Thus kindly I scatter
  Thy leaves o'er the bed,
Where thy mates of the garden
  Lie scentless and dead.

So soon may *I* follow,
　　When friendships decay,
　And from Love's shining circle
　　The gems drop away.
　When true hearts lie wither'd,
　　And fond ones are flown,
Oh! who would inhabit
　　This bleak world alone?

On Music.

When thro' life unblest we rove,
    Losing all that made life dear,
Should some notes we used to love,
    In days of boyhood, meet our ear,
Oh! how welcome breathes the strain!
    Wakening thoughts that long have slept;
Kindling former smiles again
    In faded eyes that long have wept.

Like the gale, that sighs along
    Beds of oriental flowers,
Is the grateful breath of song,
    That once was heard in happier hours;
Fill'd with balm, the gale sighs on,
    Though the flowers have sunk in death;
So, when pleasure's dream is gone,
    Its memory lives in Music's breath.

D. Maclise, R.A.   F. P. Becker.

Music, oh how faint, how weak,
 Language fades before thy spell!
Why should Feeling ever speak,
 When thou canst breathe her soul so well?
Friendship's balmy words may feign,
 Love's are ev'n more false than they;
Oh! 'tis only music's strain
 Can sweetly soothe, and not betray.

The Minstrel-Boy.

The Minstrel-Boy to the war is gone,
   In the ranks of death you'll find him;
His father's sword he has girded on,
   And his wild harp slung behind him.—
"Land of song!" said the warrior-bard,
   "Tho' all the world betrays thee,
"*One* sword, at least, thy rights shall guard,
   "*One* faithful harp shall praise thee!"

The Minstrel fell!—but the foeman's chain
Could not bring his proud soul under;
The harp he lov'd ne'er spoke again,
For he tore its chords asunder;
And said, "No chains shall sully thee,
"Thou soul of love and bravery!
"Thy songs were made for the pure and free,
"They shall never sound in slavery."

'Tis sweet to think.

'Tis sweet to think, that, where'er we rove,
    We are sure to find something blissful and dear,
And that, when we're far from the lips we love,
    We've but to make love to the lips we are near.[45]
The heart, like a tendril, accustom'd to cling,
    Let it grow where it will, cannot flourish alone,
But will lean to the nearest, and loveliest thing,
    It can twine with itself, and make closely its own.
Then oh! what pleasure, where'er we rove,
    To be sure to find something, still, that is dear,
And to know, when far from the lips we love,
    We've but to make love to the lips we are near.

'Twere a shame, when flowers around us rise,
 To make light of the rest, if the rose isn't there;
And the world's so rich in resplendent eyes,
 'Twere a pity to limit one's love to a pair.
Love's wing and the peacock's are nearly alike,
 They are both of them bright, but they're changeable too,
And, wherever a new beam of beauty can strike,
 It will tincture Love's plume with a different hue.
Then oh! what pleasure, where'er we rove,
 To be sure to find something, still, that is dear,
And to know, when far from the lips we love,
 We've but to make love to the lips we are near.

Farewell!—but whenever you welcome the hour.

Farewell!—but whenever you welcome the hour,
That awakens the night-song of mirth in your bower,
Then think of the friend who once welcom'd it too,
And forgot his own griefs to be happy with you.
His griefs may return, not a hope may remain
Of the few that have brighten'd his pathway of pain,
But he ne'er will forget the short vision, that threw
Its enchantment around him, while ling'ring with you.

And still on that evening, when pleasure fills up
To the highest top sparkle each heart and each cup,
Where'er my path lies, be it gloomy or bright,
My soul, happy friends, shall be with you that night;

Shall join in your revels, your sports, and your wiles,
And return to me, beaming all o'er with your smiles—
Too blest, if it tells me that, 'mid the gay cheer
Some kind voice had murmur'd, "I wish he were here!"

Let Fate do her worst, there are relics of joy,
Bright dreams of the past, which she cannot destroy;
Which come in the night-time of sorrow and care,
And bring back the features that joy used to wear.
Long, long be my heart with such memories fill'd!
Like the vase, in which roses have once been distill'd—
You may break, you may shatter the vase, if you will,
But the scent of the roses will hang round it still.

Oh! doubt me not.

Oh! doubt me not—the season
   Is o'er, when Folly made me rove,
And now the vestal, Reason,
   Shall watch the fire awak'd by Love.
Altho' this heart was early blown,
   And fairest hands disturb'd the tree,
They only shook some blossoms down,
   Its fruit has all been kept for thee.
Then doubt me not—the season
   Is o'er, when Folly made me rove,
And now the vestal, Reason,
   Shall watch the fire awak'd by Love.

And tho' my lute no longer
   May sing of Passion's ardent spell,
Yet, trust me, all the stronger
   I feel the bliss I do not tell.

The bee through many a garden roves,
　　And hums his lay of courtship o'er,
But when he finds the flower he loves,
　　He settles there, and hums no more.
　　Then doubt me not—the season
　　　　Is o'er, when Folly kept me free,
　　And now the vestal, Reason,
　　　　Shall guard the flame awak'd by thee.

I'd mourn the hopes.

I'd mourn the hopes that leave me,
    If thy smiles had left me too;
I'd weep when friends deceive me,
    If thou wert, like them, untrue.
But while I've thee before me,
    With heart so warm and eyes so bright,
No clouds can linger o'er me,
    That smile turns them all to light.

'Tis not in fate to harm me,
    While fate leaves thy love to me;
'Tis not in joy to charm me,
    Unless joy be shared with thee.
One minute's dream about thee
    Were worth a long, an endless year
Of waking bliss without thee,
    My own love, my only dear!

And tho' the hope be gone, love,
  That long sparkled o'er our way,
Oh! we shall journey on, love,
  More safely, without its ray.
Far better lights shall win me
  Along the path I've yet to roam:—
The mind that burns within me,
  And pure smiles from thee at home.

Thus, when the lamp that lighted
  The traveller at first goes out,
He feels awhile benighted,
  And looks round in fear and doubt.
But soon, the prospect clearing,
  By cloudless starlight on he treads,
And thinks no lamp so cheering
  As that light which Heaven sheds.

One bumper at parting!—tho' many
    Have circled the board since we met,
The fullest, the saddest of any
    Remains to be crown'd by us yet.
The sweetness that pleasure hath in it,
    Is always so slow to come forth,
That seldom, alas, till the minute
    It dies, do we know half its worth.

But come,—may our life's happy measure
    Be all of such moments made up;
They're born on the bosom of Pleasure,
    They die 'midst the tears of the cup.

As onward we journey, how pleasant
    To pause and inhabit awhile
Those few sunny spots, like the present,
    That 'mid the dull wilderness smile!
But Time, like a pitiless master,
    Cries "Onward!" and spurs the gay hours—
Ah, never doth Time travel faster,
    Than when his way lies among flowers.
But come—may our life's happy measure
    Be all of such moments made up;
They're born on the bosom of Pleasure,
    They die 'midst the tears of the cup.

We saw how the sun look'd in sinking,
    The waters beneath him how bright;
And now, let our farewell of drinking
    Resemble that farewell of light.
You saw how he finish'd, by darting
    His beam o'er a deep billow's brim—
So, fill up, let's shine at our parting,
    In full liquid glory, like him.

And oh! may our life's happy measure
　　Of moments like this be made up,
'Twas born on the bosom of Pleasure,
　　It dies 'mid the tears of the cup.

Has sorrow thy young days shaded,

Has sorrow thy young days shaded,
　　As clouds o'er the morning fleet?
Too fast have those young days faded,
　　That, even in sorrow, were sweet?
Does Time with his cold wing wither
　　Each feeling that once was dear?—
Then, child of misfortune, come hither,
　　I'll weep with thee, tear for tear.

D. Maclise, R.A.　　　　　　　　　　　　　　　　F. P. Becker.

Has love to that soul, so tender,
   Been like our Lagenian mine,[46]
Where sparkles of golden splendour
   All over the surface shine—
But, if in pursuit we go deeper,
   Allur'd by the gleam that shone,
Ah! false as the dream of the sleeper,
   Like Love, the bright ore is gone.

Has Hope, like the bird in the story,[47]
   That flitted from tree to tree
With the talisman's glittering glory—
   Has Hope been that bird to thee?
On branch after branch alighting,
   The gem did she still display,
And, when nearest and most inviting,
   Then waft the fair gem away?

If thus the young hours have fleeted,
   When sorrow itself look'd bright;
If thus the fair hope hath cheated,
   That led thee along so light;
If thus the cold world now wither
   Each feeling that once was dear:—
Come child of misfortune, come hither,
   I'll weep with thee, tear for tear.

Let fate frown on, so we love and part not;
'Tis life where *thou* art, 'tis death where thou art not.
    Then come o'er the sea,
    Maiden, with me,
Come wherever the wild wind blows;
    Seasons may roll,
    But the true soul
Burns the same, where'er it goes.

    Was not the sea
    Made for the Free,
Land for courts and chains alone?
    Here we are slaves,
    But, on the waves,
Love and Liberty's all our own.
No eye to watch, and no tongue to wound us,
All earth forgot, and all heaven around us—
    Then come o'er the sea,
    Maiden, with me,
Mine thro' sunshine, storm, and snows;
    Seasons may roll,
    But the true soul
Burns the same, where'er it goes.

When first I met Thee.

When first I met thee, warm and young,
   There shone such truth about thee,
And on thy lip such promise hung,
   I did not dare to doubt thee.
I saw thee change, yet still relied,
   Still clung with hope the fonder,
And thought, tho' false to all beside,
   From me thou couldst not wander.
     But go, deceiver! go,
        The heart, whose hopes could make it
     Trust one so false, so low,
        Deserves that thou shouldst break it.

When every tongue thy follies nam'd,
   I fled the unwelcome story;
Or found, in ev'n the faults they blam'd,
   Some gleams of future glory.

I still was true, when nearer friends
   Conspired to wrong, to slight thee;
The heart that now thy falsehood rends,
   Would then have bled to right thee.
     But go, deceiver! go,—
        Some day, perhaps, thou'lt waken
     From pleasure's dream, to know
        The grief of hearts forsaken.

Even now, tho' youth its bloom has shed,
   No lights of age adorn thee:
The few, who lov'd thee once, have fled,
   And they who flatter scorn thee.
Thy midnight cup is pledg'd to slaves,
   No genial ties enwreath it;
The smiling there, like light on graves,
   Has rank cold hearts beneath it.
     Go—go—tho' worlds were thine,
        I would not now surrender
     One taintless tear of mine
        For all thy guilty splendour!

And days may come, thou false one! yet,
   When even those ties shall sever;
When thou wilt call, with vain regret,
   On her thou'st lost for ever;

On her who, in thy fortune's fall,
   With smiles had still receiv'd thee,
And gladly died to prove thee all
   Her fancy first believ'd thee.
Go—go—'tis vain to curse,
   'Tis weakness to upbraid thee;
Hate cannot wish thee worse
   Than guilt and shame have made thee.

Where is the Slave.

Oh, where's the slave so lowly,
Condemn'd to chains unholy,
  Who, could he burst
  His bonds at first,
Would pine beneath them slowly?
What soul, whose wrongs degrade it,
Would wait till time decay'd it,
  When thus its wing
  At once may spring
To the throne of Him who made it?

Farewell, Erin,—farewell, all,
Who live to weep our fall!

Less dear the laurel growing,
Alive, untouch'd and blowing,
  Than that, whose braid
  Is pluck'd to shade
The brows with victory glowing.

We tread the land that bore us,
Her green flag glitters o'er us,
  The friends we've tried
  Are by our side,
And the foe we hate before us.

Farewell, Erin,—farewell, all,
Who live to weep our fall!

The Time I've lost in Wooing.

The time I've lost in wooing,
In watching and pursuing
  The light, that lies
  In woman's eyes,
Has been my heart's undoing.
Tho' Wisdom oft has sought me,
I scorn'd the lore she brought me,
  My only books
  Were woman's looks,
And folly's all they've taught me.

Her smile when Beauty granted,
I hung with gaze enchanted,
    Like him the Sprite,*
    Whom maids by night
Oft meet in glen that's haunted.
Like him, too, Beauty won me,
But while her eyes were on me,
    If once their ray
    Was turn'd away,
O! winds could not outrun me.

And are those follies going?
And is my proud heart growing
　　Too cold or wise
　　For brilliant eyes
Again to set it glowing?
No, vain, alas! th' endeavour
From bonds so sweet to sever;
　　Poor Wisdom's chance
　　Against a glance
Is now as weak as ever.

Fill the bumper fair.

Fill the bumper fair!
    Every drop we sprinkle
O'er the brow of Care
    Smooths away a wrinkle.
Wit's electric flame
    Ne'er so swiftly passes,
As when thro' the frame
    It shoots from brimming glasses.
Fill the bumper fair!
    Every drop we sprinkle
O'er the brow of Care
    Smooths away a wrinkle.

Sages can, they say,
    Grasp the lightning's pinions,
And bring down its ray
    From the starr'd dominions:—
So we, Sages, sit,
    And, 'mid bumpers bright'ning,
From the Heaven of Wit
    Draw down all its lightning.

Would'st thou know what first
    Made our souls inherit
This ennobling thirst
    For wine's celestial spirit?
It chanc'd upon that day,
    When, as bards inform us,
Prometheus stole away
    The living fires that warm us:

The careless Youth, when up
    To Glory's fount aspiring,
Took nor urn nor cup
    To hide the pilfer'd fire in.—
But oh his joy, when, round
    The halls of Heaven spying,
Among the stars he found
    A bowl of Bacchus lying!

Some drops were in that bowl,
    Remains of last night's pleasure,
With which the Sparks of Soul
    Mix'd their burning treasure.
Hence the goblet's shower
    Hath such spells to win us;
Hence its mighty power
    O'er that flame within us.
Fill the bumper fair!
    Every drop we sprinkle
O'er the brow of Care
    Smooths away a wrinkle.

No, not more welcome the fairy numbers
    Of music fall on the sleeper's ear,
When half-awaking from fearful slumbers,
    He thinks the full quire of heaven is near,—
Than came that voice, when, all forsaken,
    This heart long had sleeping lain,
Nor thought its cold pulse would ever waken
    To such benign, blessed sounds again.

Sweet voice of comfort! 'twas like the stealing
   Of summer wind thro' some wreathed shell—
Each secret winding, each inmost feeling
   Of all my soul echoed to its spell.
'Twas whisper'd balm—'twas sunshine spoken!—
   I'd live years of grief and pain
To have my long sleep of sorrow broken
   By such benign, blessed sounds again.

Though humble the Banquet.

Though humble the banquet to which I invite thee,
   Thou'lt find there the best a poor bard can command:
Eyes, beaming with welcome, shall throng round, to light thee,
   And Love serve the feast with his own willing hand.

D. Maclise, R.A.   F. P. Becker.

And though Fortune may seem to have turn'd from the dwelling
  Of him thou regardest her favouring ray,
Thou wilt find there a gift, all her treasures excelling,
  Which, proudly he feels, hath ennobled his way.

'Tis that freedom of mind, which no vulgar dominion
  Can turn from the path a pure conscience approves;
Which, with hope in the heart, and no chain on the pinion,
  Holds upwards its course to the light which it loves.

'Tis this makes the pride of his humble retreat,
  And, with this, though of all other treasures bereaved,
The breeze of his garden to him is more sweet
  Than the costliest incense that Pomp e'er received.

Then, come,—if a board so untempting hath power
  To win thee from grandeur, its best shall be thine;
And there's one, long the light of the bard's happy bower,
  Who, smiling, will blend her bright welcome with mine.

D. Maclise, R.A. E. P. Becker.

They know not my Heart.

They know not my heart, who believe there can be
One stain of this earth in its feelings for thee;
Who think, while I see thee in beauty's young hour,
As pure as the morning's first dew on the flow'r,
I could harm what I love,—as the sun's wanton ray
But smiles on the dew-drop to waste it away.

No—beaming with light as those young features are,
There's a light round thy heart which is lovelier far:
It *is* not that cheek—'tis the soul dawning clear
Thro' its innocent blush makes thy beauty so dear;
As the sky we look up to, though glorious and fair,
Is look'd up to the more, because Heaven lies there!

D. Maclise, R.A. F. P. Becker.

While History's Muse the memorial was keeping
Of all that the dark hand of Destiny weaves,
Beside her the Genius of Erin stood weeping,
For hers was the story that blotted the leaves,
But oh! how the tear in her eyelids grew bright,
When, after whole pages of sorrow and shame,
She saw History write,
With a pencil of light
That illum'd the whole volume, her Wellington's name.

D. Maclise, R.A. F. P. Becker.

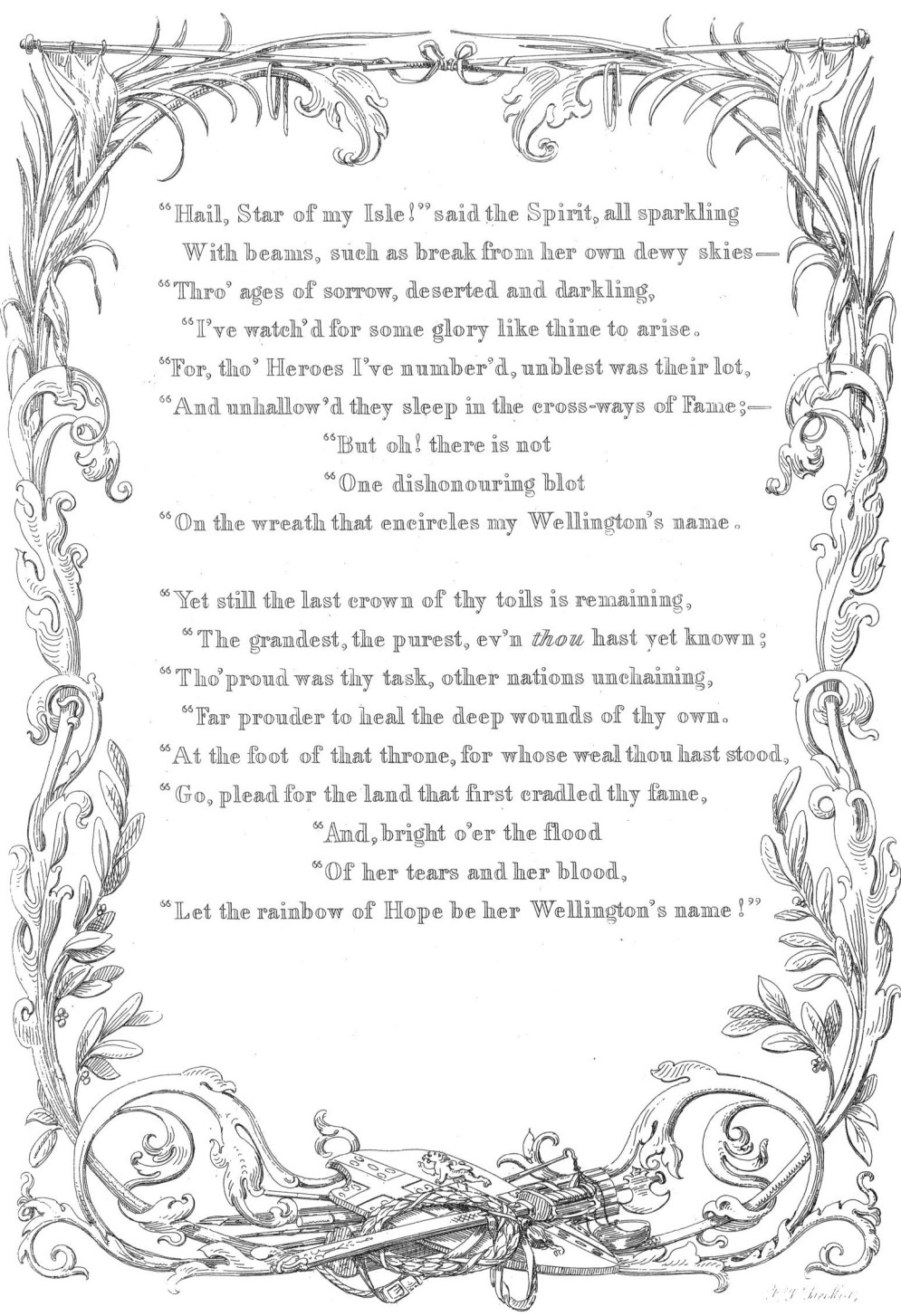

"Hail, Star of my Isle!" said the Spirit, all sparkling
    With beams, such as break from her own dewy skies—
"Thro' ages of sorrow, deserted and darkling,
    "I've watch'd for some glory like thine to arise.
"For, tho' Heroes I've number'd, unblest was their lot,
    "And unhallow'd they sleep in the cross-ways of Fame;—
        "But oh! there is not
        "One dishonouring blot
"On the wreath that encircles my Wellington's name.

"Yet still the last crown of thy toils is remaining,
    "The grandest, the purest, ev'n *thou* hast yet known;
"Tho' proud was thy task, other nations unchaining,
    "Far prouder to heal the deep wounds of thy own.
"At the foot of that throne, for whose weal thou hast stood,
"Go, plead for the land that first cradled thy fame,
        "And, bright o'er the flood
        "Of her tears and her blood,
"Let the rainbow of Hope be her Wellington's name!"

'Tis gone, and for ever,

'Tis gone, and for ever, the light we saw breaking,
　　Like Heaven's first dawn o'er the sleep of the dead—
When Man, from the slumber of ages awaking,
　　Look'd upward, and bless'd the pure ray, ere it fled.
'Tis gone, and the gleams it has left of its burning
But deepen the long night of bondage and mourning,
That dark o'er the kingdoms of earth is returning,
　　And darkest of all, hapless Erin, o'er thee.

For high was thy hope, when those glories were darting
　　Around thee, thro' all the gross clouds of the world;
When Truth, from her fetters indignantly starting,
　　At once, like a Sun-burst, her banner unfurl'd.[49]

Oh! never shall earth see a moment so splendid!
Then, then—had one Hymn of Deliverance blended
The tongues of all nations—how sweet had ascended
    The first note of Liberty, Erin, from thee!

But, shame on those tyrants, who envied the blessing!
    And shame on the light race, unworthy its good,
Who, at Death's reeking altar, like furies, caressing
    The young hope of Freedom, baptiz'd it in blood.
Then vanish'd for ever that fair, sunny vision,
Which, spite of the slavish, the cold heart's derision,
Shall long be remember'd, pure, bright, and elysian,
    As first it arose, my lost Erin, on thee.

D. Maclise, R.A.   F. P. Becker.

Come, rest in this bosom, my own stricken deer,
Tho' the herd have fled from thee, thy home is still here;
Here still is the smile, that no cloud can o'ercast,
And a heart and a hand all thy own to the last.

Oh! what was love made for, if 'tis not the same
Thro' joy and thro' torment, thro' glory and shame?
I know not, I ask not, if guilt's in that heart,
I but know that I love thee, whatever thou art.

Thou hast call'd me thy Angel in moments of bliss,
And thy Angel I'll be, 'mid the horrors of this,—
Thro' the furnace, unshrinking, thy steps to pursue,
And shield thee, and save thee,—or perish there too!

Forget not the Field.

Forget not the field where they perish'd,
    The truest, the last of the brave,
All gone—and the bright hope we cherish'd
    Gone with them, and quench'd in their grave!

Oh! could we from death but recover
    Those hearts as they bounded before,
In the face of high heav'n to fight over
    That combat for freedom once more;—

Could the chain for an instant be riven
    Which Tyranny flung round us then,
No, 'tis not in Man, nor in Heaven,
    To let Tyranny bind it again!

But 'tis past—and, tho' blazon'd in story
    The name of our Victor may be,
Accurst is the march of that glory
    Which treads o'er the hearts of the free.

Far dearer the grave or the prison,
    Illumed by one patriot name,
Than the trophies of all, who have risen
    On Liberty's ruins to fame.

My gentle Harp.

My gentle Harp, once more I waken
    The sweetness of thy slumbering strain;
In tears our last farewell was taken,
    And now in tears we meet again.
No light of joy hath o'er thee broken,
    But, like those Harps whose heav'nly skill
Of slavery, dark as thine, hath spoken,
    Thou hang'st upon the willows still.

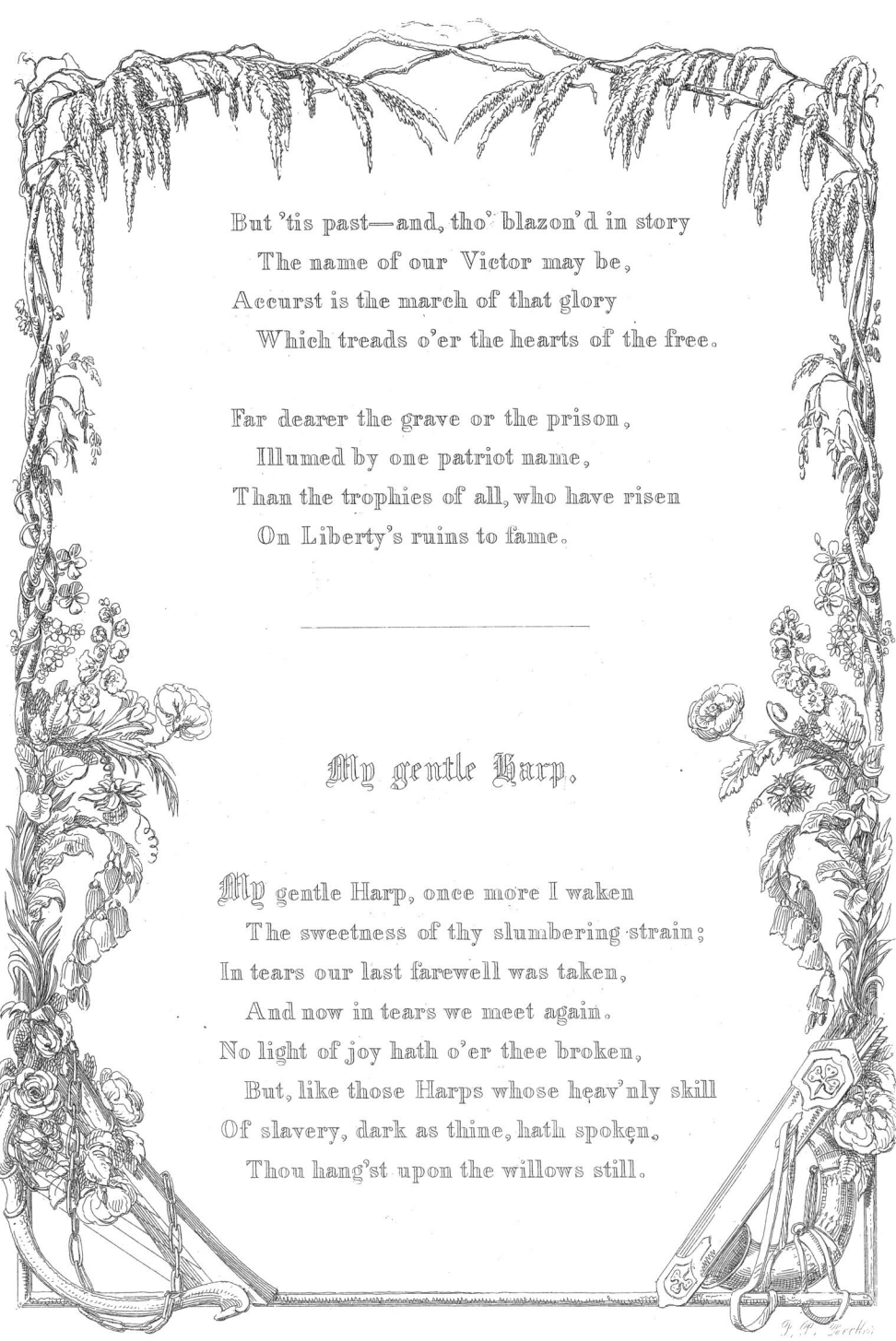

And yet, since last thy chord resounded,
   An hour of peace and triumph came,
And many an ardent bosom bounded
   With hopes—that now are turn'd to shame.
Yet even then, while Peace was singing
   Her halcyon song o'er land and sea,
Tho' joy and hope to others bringing,
   She only brought new tears to thee.

Then, who can ask for notes of pleasure,
   My drooping Harp, from chords like thine?
Alas, the lark's gay morning measure
   As ill would suit the swan's decline!
Or how shall I, who love, who bless thee,
   Invoke thy breath for Freedom's strains,
When ev'n the wreaths in which I dress thee,
   Are sadly mix'd—half flow'rs, half chains?

But come—if yet thy frame can borrow
   One breath of joy, oh, breathe for me,
And show the world, in chains and sorrow,
   How sweet thy music still can be;
How gaily, ev'n mid gloom surrounding,
   Thou yet canst wake at pleasure's thrill—
Like Memnon's broken image sounding,
   'Mid desolation tuneful still!

As slow our ship her foamy track
  Against the wind was cleaving,
Her trembling pennant still look'd back
  To that dear isle 'twas leaving.
So loath we part from all we love,
  From all the links that bind us;
So turn our hearts as on we rove,
  To those we've left behind us.

When, round the bowl, of vanish'd years
   We talk, with joyous seeming,—
With smiles that might as well be tears,
   So faint, so sad their beaming;
While mem'ry brings us back again
   Each early tie that twined us,
Oh, sweet's the cup that circles then
   To those we've left behind us.

And when, in other climes, we meet
   Some isle, or vale enchanting,
Where all looks flow'ry, wild, and sweet,
   And nought but love is wanting;
We think how great had been our bliss,
   If Heav'n had but assign'd us
To live and die in scenes like this,
   With some we've left behind us!

As trav'llers oft look back at eve,
   When eastward darkly going,
To gaze upon that light they leave
   Still faint behind them glowing,—
So, when the close of pleasure's day
   To gloom hath near consign'd us,
We turn to catch one fading ray
   Of joy that's left behind us.

In the Morning of Life.

In the morning of life, when its cares are unknown,
    And its pleasures in all their new lustre begin,
When we live in a bright-beaming world of our own,
    And the light that surrounds us is all from within;
Oh 'tis not, believe me, in that happy time
    We can love, as in hours of less transport we may;—
Of our smiles, of our hopes, 'tis the gay sunny prime,
    But affection is truest when these fade away.

When we see the first glory of youth pass us by,
    Like a leaf on the stream that will never return;
When our cup, which had sparkled with pleasure so high,
    First tastes of the *other*, the dark-flowing urn;
Then, then is the time when affection holds sway
    With a depth and a tenderness joy never knew;
Love, nursed among pleasures, is faithless as they,
    But the love born of Sorrow, like Sorrow, is true.

D. Maclise, R.A.   F. P. Becker.

In climes full of sunshine, though splendid the flowers,
 Their sighs have no freshness, their odour no worth;
'Tis the cloud and the mist of our own Isle of showers,
 That call the rich spirit of fragrancy forth.
So it is not 'mid splendour, prosperity, mirth,
 That the depth of Love's generous spirit appears;
To the sunshine of smiles it may first owe its birth,
 But the soul of its sweetness is drawn out by tears.

When cold in the earth lies the friend thou hast loved,
  Be his faults and his follies forgot by thee then;
Or, if from their slumber the veil be removed,
  Weep o'er them in silence, and close it again.
And oh! if 'tis pain to remember how far
  From the pathways of light he was tempted to roam,
Be it bliss to remember that thou wert the star
  That arose on his darkness, and guided him home.

From thee and thy innocent beauty first came
  The revealings, that taught him true love to adore,
To feel the bright presence, and turn him with shame
  From the idols he blindly had knelt to before.
O'er the waves of a life, long benighted and wild,
  Thou camest, like a soft golden calm o'er the sea;
And if happiness purely and glowingly smiled
  On his ev'ning horizon, the light was from thee.

And tho', sometimes, the shades of past folly might rise,
  And tho' falsehood again would allure him to stray,
He but turn'd to the glory that dwelt in those eyes,
  And the folly, the falsehood, soon vanish'd away.
As the Priests of the Sun, when their altar grew dim,
  At the day-beam alone could its lustre repair,
So, if virtue a moment grew languid in him,
  He but flew to that smile and rekindled it there.

To Ladies' Eyes.

To Ladies' eyes around, boy,
   We can't refuse, we can't refuse,
Tho' bright eyes so abound, boy,
   'Tis hard to choose, 'tis hard to choose.
For thick as stars that lighten
   Yon airy bow'rs, yon airy bow'rs,
The countless eyes that brighten
   This earth of ours, this earth of ours.
But fill the cup—where'er, boy,
   Our choice may fall, our choice may fall,
We're sure to find Love there, boy,
   So drink them all! so drink them all!

Some looks there are so holy,
   They seem but giv'n, they seem but giv'n,
As shining beacons, solely,
   To light to heav'n, to light to heav'n.

While some—oh! ne'er believe them—
    With tempting ray, with tempting ray,
Would lead us (God forgive them!)
    The other way, the other way.
But fill the cup—where'er, boy,
    Our choice may fall, our choice may fall,
We're sure to find Love there, boy,
    So drink them all! so drink them all!

In some, as in a mirror,
    Love seems pourtray'd, Love seems pourtray'd,
But shun the flattering error,
    'Tis but his shade, 'tis but his shade.
Himself has fix'd his dwelling
    In eyes we know, in eyes we know,
And lips—but this is telling—
    So here they go! so here they go!
Fill up, fill up—where'er, boy,
    Our choice may fall, our choice may fall,
We're sure to find Love there, boy,
    So drink them all! so drink them all!

Wreath the bowl
    With flowers of soul,
The brightest Wit can find us;
    We'll take a flight
    Tow'rds heaven to-night,
And leave dull earth behind us.
    Should Love amid
    The wreaths be hid,
That joy, th'enchanter, brings us,
    No danger fear,
    While wine is near,
We'll drown him if he stings us.

Then, wreath the bowl
With flowers of soul,
The brightest Wit can find us;
We'll take a flight
Tow'rds heaven to-night,
And leave dull earth behind us.

'Twas nectar fed
Of old, 'tis said,
Their Junos, Joves, Apollos;
And man may brew
His nectar too,
The rich receipt's as follows:
Take wine like this,
Let looks of bliss
Around it well be blended,
Then bring Wit's beam
To warm the stream,
And there's your nectar, splendid!
So wreath the bowl
With flowers of soul,
The brightest Wit can find us;
We'll take a flight
Tow'rds heaven to-night,
And leave dull earth behind us.

Say, why did Time
His glass sublime
Fill up with sands unsightly,
When wine, he knew,
Runs brisker through,
And sparkles far more brightly?
Oh, lend it us,
And, smiling thus,
The glass in two we'll sever,
Make pleasure glide
In double tide,
And fill both ends for ever!
Then wreath the bowl
With flowers of soul
The brightest Wit can find us;
We'll take a flight
Tow'rds heaven to-night,
And leave dull earth behind us.

They may rail at this Life.

They may rail at this life—from the hour I began it,
  I found it a life full of kindness and bliss;
And, until they can show me some happier planet,
  More social and bright, I'll content me with this.
As long as the world has such lips and such eyes,
  As before me this moment enraptured I see,
They may say what they will of their orbs in the skies,
  But this earth is the planet for you, love, and me.

In Mercury's star, where each moment can bring them
  New sunshine and wit from the fountain on high,
Tho' the nymphs may have livelier poets to sing them,
  They've none, even there, more enamour'd than I.
And, as long as this harp can be waken'd to love,
  And that eye its divine inspiration shall be,
They may talk as they will of their Edens above,
  But this earth is the planet for you, love, and me.

In that star of the west, by whose shadowy splendour,
At twilight so often we've roam'd through the dew,
There are maidens, perhaps, who have bosoms as tender,
And look, in their twilights, as lovely as you.

But tho' they were even more bright than the queen
    Of that isle they inhabit in heaven's blue sea,
As I never those fair young celestials have seen,
    Why—this earth is the planet for you, love, and me.

As for those chilly orbs on the verge of creation,
    Where sunshine and smiles must be equally rare,
Did they want a supply of cold hearts for that station,
    Heav'n knows we have plenty on earth we could spare.

Oh! think what a world we should have of it here,
    If the haters of peace, of affection and glee,
Were to fly up to Saturn's comfortless sphere,
    And leave earth to such spirits as you, love, and me.

D. Maclise, R.A.   F. P. Becker.

Ne'er ask the Hour.

Ne'er ask the hour—what is it to us
    How Time deals out his treasures?
The golden moments lent us thus,
    Are not *his* coin, but Pleasure's.
If counting them o'er could add to their blisses,
    I'd number each glorious second:
But moments of joy are, like Lesbia's kisses,
    Too quick and sweet to be reckon'd.
Then fill the cup—what is it to us
    How time his circle measures?
The fairy hours we call up thus,
    Obey no wand but Pleasure's.

Young Joy ne'er thought of counting hours,
    Till Care, one summer's morning,
Set up, among his smiling flowers,
    A dial, by way of warning,

D. Maclise, R.A.   F. P. Becker.

But Joy loved better to gaze on the sun,
    As long as its light was glowing,
Than to watch with old Care how the shadow stole on,
    And how fast that light was going.
So fill the cup—what is it to us
    How Time his circle measures?
The fairy hours we call up thus,
    Obey no wand but Pleasure's.

If thou'lt be mine.

If thou'lt be mine, the treasures of air,
    Of earth, and sea, shall lie at thy feet;
Whatever in Fancy's eye looks fair,
    Or in Hope's sweet music sounds *most* sweet,
      Shall be ours—if thou wilt be mine, love!

Bright flowers shall bloom wherever we rove,
    A voice divine shall talk in each stream;
The stars shall look like worlds of love,
    And this earth be all one beautiful dream
      In our eyes—if thou wilt be mine, love!

And thoughts, whose source is hidden and high,
    Like streams, that come from heaven-ward hills,
Shall keep our hearts, like meads, that lie
    To be bathed by those eternal rills,
      Ever green, if thou wilt be mine, love!

All this and more the Spirit of Love
    Can breathe o'er them, who feel his spells;
That heaven, which forms his home above,
    He can make on earth, wherever he dwells,
      As thou'lt own,—if thou wilt be mine, love!

Whene'er I see those smiling eyes.

Whene'er I see those smiling eyes,
   So full of hope, and joy, and light,
As if no cloud could ever rise,
   To dim a heav'n so purely bright—
I sigh to think how soon that brow
   In grief may lose its every ray,
And that light heart, so joyous now,
   Almost forget it once was gay.

For time will come with all its blights,
   The ruined hope, the friend unkind,
And love, that leaves, where'er it lights,
   A chill'd or burning heart behind:—
While youth, that now like snow appears,
   Ere sullied by the dark'ning rain,
When once 'tis touch'd by sorrow's tears
   Can never shine so bright again.

Oh for the swords of former time!

Oh for the swords of former time!
　　Oh for the men who bore them,
When arm'd for Right, they stood sublime,
　　And tyrants crouch'd before them:
When free yet, ere courts began
　　With honours to enslave him,
The best honours worn by Man
　　Were those which Virtue gave him.
Oh for the swords, &c. &c.

Oh for the Kings who flourish'd then!
　　Oh for the pomp that crown'd them,
When hearts and hands of freeborn men
　　Were all the ramparts round them.
When, safe built on bosoms true,
　　The throne was but the centre,
Round which Love a circle drew,
　　That Treason durst not enter.
Oh for the Kings who flourish'd then!
　　Oh for the pomp that crown'd them,
When hearts and hands of freeborn men
　　Were all the ramparts round them!

Sail on, sail on.

Sail on, sail on, thou fearless bark—
    Wherever blows the welcome wind,
It cannot lead to scenes more dark,
    More sad than those we leave behind.
Each wave that passes seems to say,
    "Though death beneath our smile may be,
"Less cold we are, less false than they,
    "Whose smiling wreck'd thy hopes and thee."

Sail on, sail on, through endless space—
    Through calm—through tempest—stop no more:
The stormiest sea's a resting place
    To him who leaves such hearts on shore.
Or—if some desert land we meet,
    Where never yet false-hearted men
Profaned a world, that else were sweet,—
    Then rest thee, bark, but not till then.

The Parallel.

Yes, sad one of Sion, if closely resembling,"
    In shame and in sorrow, thy wither'd-up heart —
If drinking deep, deep, of the same "cup of trembling"
    Could make us thy children, our parent thou art.

Like thee doth our nation lie conquer'd and broken,
    And fall'n from her head is the once royal crown;
In her streets, in her halls, Desolation hath spoken,
    And "while it is day yet, her sun hath gone down."

Like thine doth her exile, 'mid dreams of returning,
    Die far from the home it were life to behold;
Like thine do her sons, in the day of their mourning,
    Remember the bright things that bless'd them of old.

Ah, well may we call her, like thee "the Forsaken,"⁵⁵
    Her boldest are vanquish'd, her proudest are slaves;
And the harps of her minstrels, when gayest they waken,
    Have tones 'mid their mirth like the wind over graves!

Yet hadst thou thy vengeance—yet came there the morrow,
    That shines out, at last, on the longest dark night,
When the sceptre, that smote thee with slavery and sorrow,
    Was shiver'd at once, like a reed, in thy sight.

When that cup, which for others the proud Golden City⁵⁶
    Had brimm'd full of bitterness, drench'd her own lips;
And the world she had trampled on heard, without pity,
    The howl in her halls, and the cry from her ships.

When the curse Heaven keeps for the haughty came over
    Her merchants rapacious, her rulers unjust,
And, a ruin, at last, for the earthworm to cover,⁵⁷
    The Lady of Kingdoms lay low in the dust.⁵⁸

D. Maclise, R.A.   F. P. Becker.

Drink of this cup.

Drink of this cup;—you'll find there's a spell in
    Its every drop 'gainst the ills of mortality;
Talk of the cordial that sparkled for Helen!
    Her cup was a fiction, but this is reality.
Would you forget the dark world we are in,
    Just taste of the bubble that gleams on the top of it;
But would you rise above earth, till akin
    To Immortals themselves, you must drain every drop of it;
Send round the cup—for oh there's a spell in
    Its every drop 'gainst the ills of mortality;
Talk of the cordial that sparkled for Helen!
    Her cup was a fiction, but this is reality.

Never was philter form'd with such power
    To charm and bewilder as this we are quaffing;
Its magic began when, in Autumn's rich hour,
    A harvest of gold in the fields it stood laughing.

D. Maclise, R.A.   F. P. Becker.

There having, by Nature's enchantment, been fill'd
    With the balm and the bloom of her kindliest weather,
This wonderful juice from its core was distill'd
    To enliven such hearts as are here brought together.
Then drink of the cup—you'll find there's a spell in
    Its every drop 'gainst the ills of mortality;
Talk of the cordial that sparkled for Helen!
    Her cup was a fiction, but this is reality.

And though, perhaps—but breathe it to no one—
    Like liquor the witch brews at midnight so awful,
This philter in secret was first taught to flow on,
    Yet 'tis n't less potent for being unlawful.
And, ev'n though it taste of the smoke of that flame,
    Which in silence extracted its virtue forbidden—
Fill up—there's a fire in some hearts I could name,
    Which may work too its charm, though as lawless and
        hidden.
So drink of the cup—for oh there's a spell in
    Its every drop 'gainst the ills of mortality;
Talk of the cordial that sparkled for Helen!
    Her cup was a fiction, but this is reality.

Oh, ye Dead! oh, ye Dead! whom we know by the
    light you give
From your cold gleaming eyes, though you move
    like men who live,
    Why leave you thus your graves,
    In far off fields and waves,
Where the worm and the sea-bird only know your bed,
    To haunt this spot where all
    Those eyes that wept your fall,
And the hearts that wail'd you, like your own, lie dead?

It is true, it is true, we are shadows cold and wan;
And the fair and the brave whom we lov'd on earth are gone;
But still thus ev'n in death;
So sweet the living breath
Of the fields and the flowers in our youth we wander'd o'er,
That ere, condemn'd, we go
To freeze 'mid Hecla's snow,
We would taste it awhile, and think we live once more!

The Fortune-teller.

Down in the valley come meet me to-night,
And I'll tell you your fortune truly
As ever 'twas told, by the new-moon's light,
To a young maiden, shining as newly.

But, for the world, let no one be nigh,
    Lest haply the stars should deceive me;
Such secrets between you and me and the sky
    Should never go farther, believe me.

If at that hour the heav'ns be not dim,
    My science shall call up before you
A male apparition,—the image of him
    Whose destiny 'tis to adore you.

And if to that phantom you'll be kind,
    So fondly around you he'll hover,
You'll hardly, my dear, any difference find
    'Twixt him and a true living lover.

Down at your feet, in the pale moonlight,
    He'll kneel, with a warmth of devotion—
An ardour, of which such an innocent sprite
    You'd scarcely believe had a notion.

What other thoughts and events may arise,
    As in destiny's book I've not seen them,
Must only be left to the stars and your eyes
    To settle, ere morning, between them.

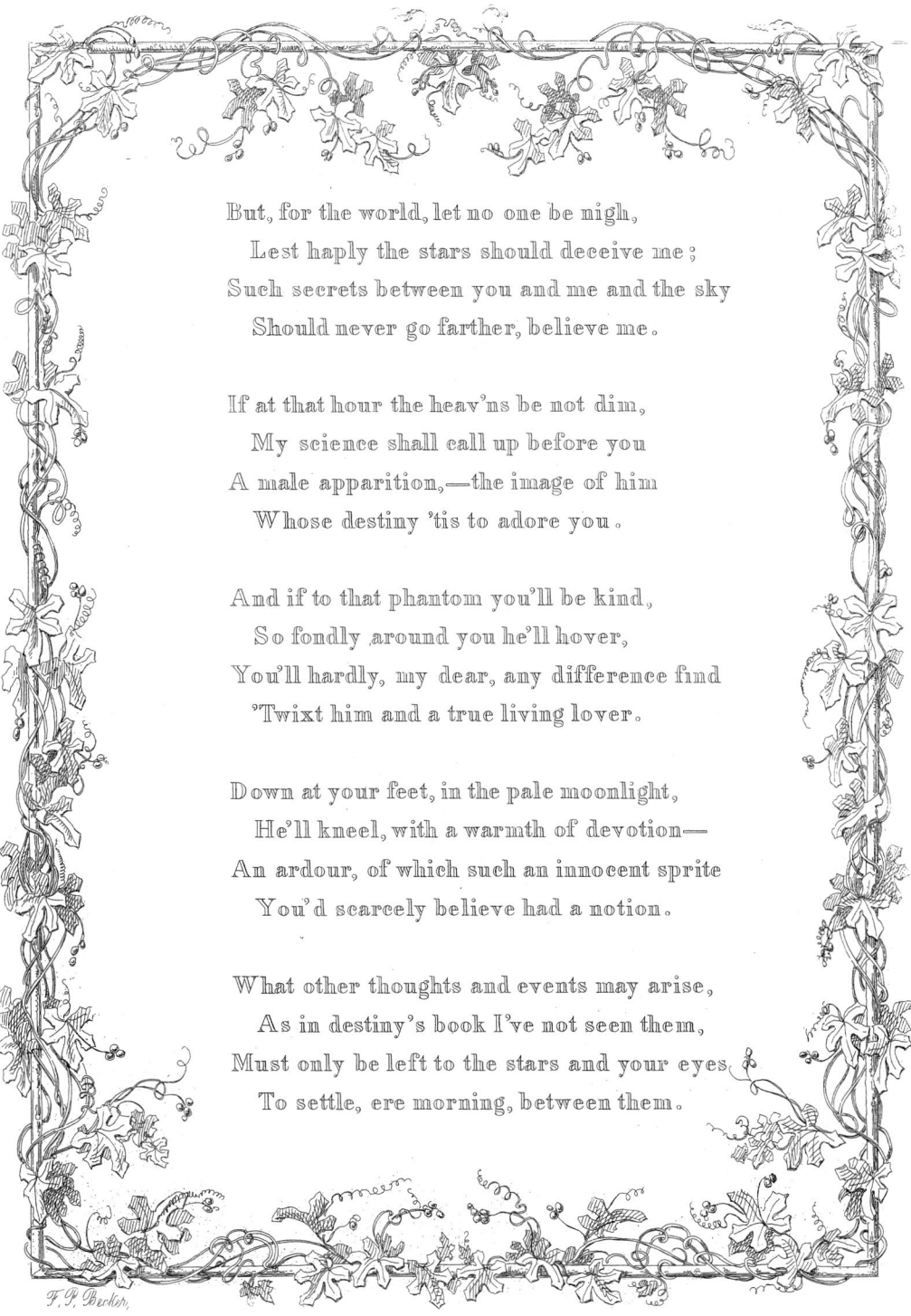

Oh banquet not.

Oh banquet not in those shining bowers,
  Where Youth resorts, but come to me:
For mine's a garden of faded flowers,
  More fit for sorrow, for age, and thee.
And there we shall have our feast of tears,
  And many a cup in silence pour;
Our guests, the shades of former years,
  Our toasts, to lips that bloom no more.

There, while the myrtle's withering boughs
  Their lifeless leaves around us shed,
We'll brim the bowl to broken vows,
  To friends long lost, the changed, the dead.
Or, while some blighted laurel waves
  Its branches o'er the dreary spot,
We'll drink to those neglected graves,
  Where valour sleeps, unnamed, forgot!

Echo.

How sweet the answer Echo makes
    To music at night,
When, roused by lute or horn, she wakes,
And far away, o'er lawns and lakes,
    Goes answering light.

Yet Love hath echoes truer far,
    And far more sweet,
Than e'er beneath the moonlight's star,
Of horn or lute, or soft guitar,
    The songs repeat.

'Tis when the sigh, in youth sincere,
    And only then,—
The sigh that's breath'd for one to hear,
Is by that one, that only dear,
    Breathed back again!

D. Maclise, R.A.   F. P. Becker.

Thee, thee, only thee.

The dawning of morn, the daylight's sinking,
The night's long hours still find me thinking
    Of thee, thee, only thee.
When friends are met, and goblets crown'd,
    And smiles are near, that once enchanted,
Unreach'd by all that sunshine round,
    My soul, like some dark spot, is haunted
    By thee, thee, only thee.

Whatever in fame's high path, could waken
My spirit once, is now forsaken
    For thee, thee, only thee.
Like shores, by which some headlong bark
    To th' ocean hurries, resting never,
Life's scenes go by me, bright or dark,
    I know not, heed not, hastening ever
    To thee, thee, only thee.

I have not a joy but of thy bringing,
And pain itself seems sweet when springing
    From thee, thee, only thee.
Like spells, that nought on earth can break,
    Till lips, that know the charm, have spoken,
This heart, howe'er the world may wake
    Its grief, its scorn, can but be broken
        By thee, thee, only thee.

Quick! we have but a second.

Quick! we have but a second,
    Fill round the cup, while you may;
For Time, the churl, hath beckon'd,
    And we must away, away!
Grasp the pleasure that's flying,
    For oh, not Orpheus' strain
Could keep sweet hours from dying,
    Or charm them to life again.
    Then, quick! we have but a second,
        Fill round the cup, while you may;
    For Time, the churl, hath beckon'd,
        And we must away, away!

See the glass, how it flushes,
    Like some young Hebe's lip,
And half meets thine, and blushes
    That thou shouldst delay to sip.

D. Maclise, R.A.   E.P. Becker.

Shame, oh shame unto thee,
If ever thou see'st that day,
When a cup or a lip shall woo thee,
And turn untouch'd away!
Then, quick! we have but a second,
Fill round, fill round, while you may;
For Time, the churl, hath beckon'd,
And we must away, away!

I wish I was by that dim Lake.

I wish I was by that dim Lake,
Where sinful souls their farewell take
Of this vain world, and half-way lie
In death's cold shadow, ere they die.
There, there, far from thee,
Deceitful world, my home should be;
Where, come what might of gloom and pain,
False hope should ne'er deceive again.

The lifeless sky, the mournful sound
Of unseen waters falling round;
The dry leaves, quiv'ring o'er my head,
Like man, unquiet ev'n when dead!
These, ay, these shall wean
My soul from life's deluding scene,
And turn each thought, o'ercharged with gloom,
Like willows, downward tow'rds the tomb.

As they, who to their couch at night
Would win repose, first quench the light,
So must the hopes, that keep this breast
Awake, be quench'd, ere it can rest.
Cold, cold, this heart must grow,
Unmoved by either joy or woe,
Like freezing founts, where all that's thrown
Within their current turns to stone.

Sweet Innisfallen.

Sweet Innisfallen, fare thee well,
    May calm and sunshine long be thine!
How fair thou art let others tell,—
    To *feel* how fair shall long be mine.

Sweet Innisfallen, long shall dwell
    In memory's dream that sunny smile,
Which o'er thee on that evening fell
    When first I saw thy fairy isle.

'Twas light, indeed, too blest for one,
    Who had to turn to paths of care—
Through crowded haunts again to run,
    And leave thee bright and silent there;

No more unto thy shores to come,
    But, on the world's rude ocean tost,
Dream of thee sometimes, as a home
    Of sunshine he had seen and lost.

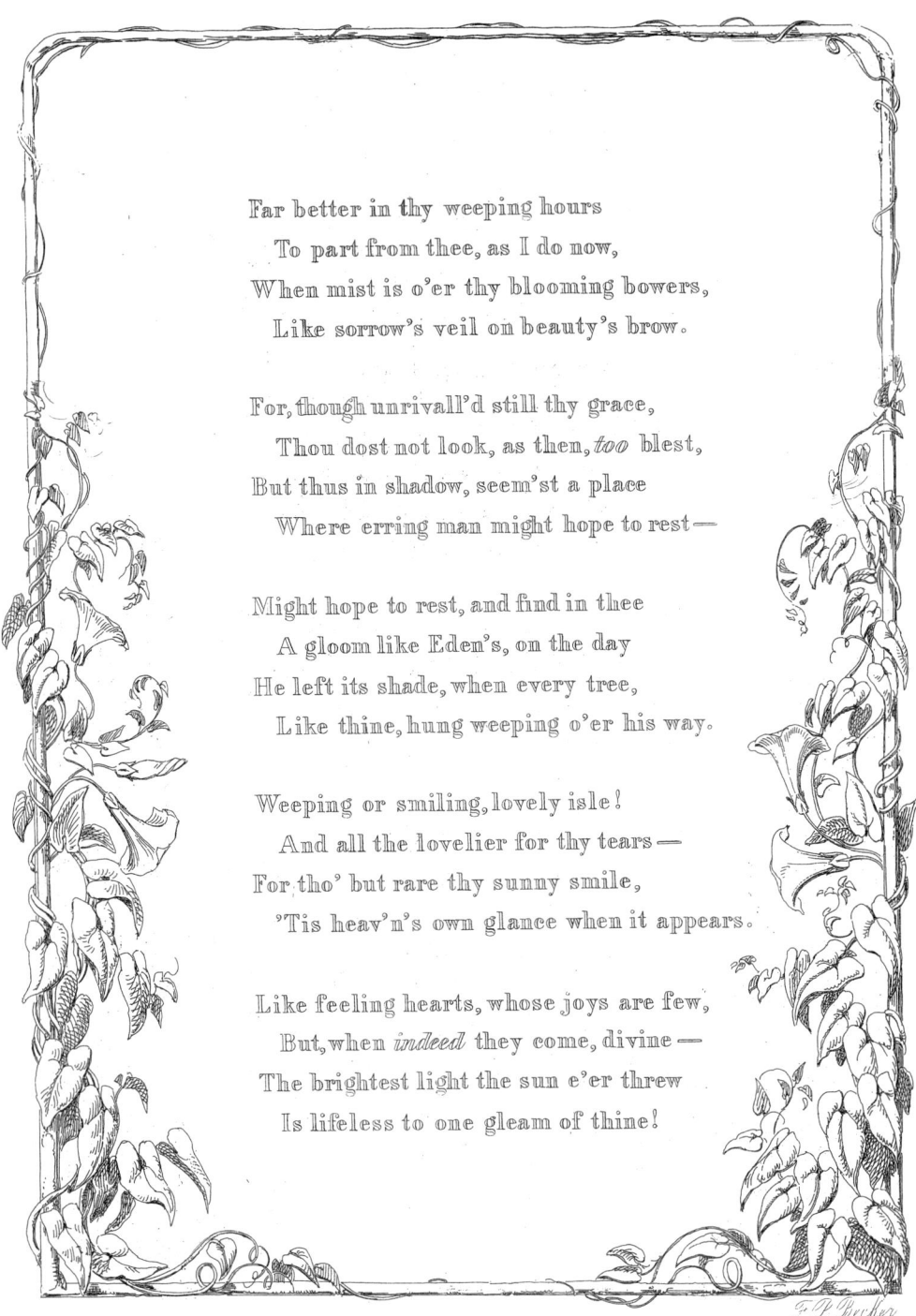

Far better in thy weeping hours
    To part from thee, as I do now,
When mist is o'er thy blooming bowers,
    Like sorrow's veil on beauty's brow.

For, though unrivall'd still thy grace,
    Thou dost not look, as then, *too* blest,
But thus in shadow, seem'st a place
    Where erring man might hope to rest—

Might hope to rest, and find in thee
    A gloom like Eden's, on the day
He left its shade, when every tree,
    Like thine, hung weeping o'er his way.

Weeping or smiling, lovely isle!
    And all the lovelier for thy tears—
For tho' but rare thy sunny smile,
    'Tis heav'n's own glance when it appears.

Like feeling hearts, whose joys are few,
    But, when *indeed* they come, divine—
The brightest light the sun e'er threw
    Is lifeless to one gleam of thine!

Oh, the sight entrancing,
When morning's beam is glancing
    O'er files array'd
    With helm and blade,
And plumes, in the gay wind dancing
When hearts are all high beating,
And the trumpet's voice repeating
    That song, whose breath
    May lead to death,
But never to retreating.

Oh the sight entrancing,
When morning's beam is glancing
    O'er files array'd
    With helm and blade,
And plumes, in the gay wind dancing.

Yet, 'tis not helm or feather—
For ask yon despot, whether
    His plumed bands
    Could bring such hands
And hearts as ours together.
Leave pomps to those who need 'em—
Give man but heart and freedom,
    And proud he braves
    The gaudiest slaves
That crawl where monarchs lead 'em.
The sword may pierce the beaver,
Stone walls in time may sever,
    'Tis mind alone,
    Worth steel and stone,
That keeps men free for ever.
Oh that sight entrancing,
When the morning's beam is glancing,
    O'er files array'd
    With helm and blade,
And in Freedom's cause advancing!

'Twas one of those Dreams.

'Twas one of those dreams, that by music are brought,
Like a bright summer haze, o'er the poet's warm thought—
When, lost in the future, his soul wanders on,
And all of this life, but its sweetness, is gone.

The wild notes he heard o'er the water were those
He had taught to sing Erin's dark bondage and woes,
And the breath of the bugle now wafted them o'er
From Dinis' green isle, to Glena's wooded shore.

He listen'd—while, high o'er the eagle's rude nest,
The lingering sounds on their way loved to rest;
And the echoes sung back from their full mountain quire,
As if loth to let song so enchanting expire.

It seem'd as if ev'ry sweet note, that died here,
Was again brought to life in some airier sphere,
Some heav'n in those hills, where the soul of the strain
That had ceased upon earth was awaking again!

Oh forgive, if, while listening to music, whose breath
Seem'd to circle his name with a charm against death,
He should feel a proud Spirit within him proclaim,
"Even so shalt thou live in the echoes of Fame:

"Even so, tho' thy memory should now die away,
"'Twill be caught up again in some happier day,
"And the hearts and the voices of Erin prolong,
"Through the answering Future, thy name and thy song.

Fairest! put on awhile.

Fairest! put on awhile
  These pinions of light I bring thee,
And o'er thy own green isle
  In fancy let me wing thee.
Never did Ariel's plume,
  At golden sunset hover
O'er scenes so full of bloom,
  As I shall waft thee over.

Fields, where the Spring delays,
  And fearlessly meets the ardour
Of the warm Summer's gaze,
  With only her tears to guard her.
Rocks, through myrtle boughs,
  In grace majestic frowning;
Like some bold warrior's brows
  That Love hath just been crowning.

Islets, so freshly fair,
  That never hath bird come nigh them,
But from his course thro' air
  He hath been won down by them;—[62]
Types, sweet maid, of thee,
  Whose look, whose blush inviting,
Never did Love yet see
  From Heav'n, without alighting.

Lakes, where the pearl lies hid,[63]
  And caves, where the gem is sleeping,
Bright as the tears thy lid
  Lets fall in lonely weeping.
Glens,[64] where Ocean comes,
  To 'scape the wild wind's rancour,
And Harbours, worthiest homes
  Where Freedom's fleet can anchor.

Then, if, while scenes so grand,
  So beautiful, shine before thee,
Pride for thy own dear land
  Should haply be stealing o'er thee,
Oh, let grief come first,
  O'er pride itself victorious—
Thinking how man hath curst
  What Heaven had made so glorious!

And doth not a Meeting like this.

And doth not a meeting like this make amends,
    For all the long years I've been wand'ring away—
To see thus around me my youth's early friends,
    As smiling and kind as in that happy day?
Though haply o'er some of your brows, as o'er mine,
    The snow-fall of time may be stealing—what then?
Like Alps in the sunset, thus lighted by wine,
    We'll wear the gay tinge of youth's roses again.

What soften'd remembrances come o'er the heart,
    In gazing on those we've been lost to so long!
The sorrows, the joys, of which once they were part,
    Still round them, like visions of yesterday, throng.
As letters some hand hath invisibly traced,
    When held to the flame will steal out on the sight,
So many a feeling, that long seem'd effaced,
    The warmth of a moment like this brings to light.

And thus, as in memory's bark we shall glide,
   To visit the scenes of our boyhood anew,
Tho' oft we may see, looking down on the tide,
   The wreck of full many a hope shining through;
Yet still, as in fancy we point to the flowers,
   That once made a garden of all the gay shore,
Deceived for a moment, we'll think them still ours,
   And breathe the fresh air of life's morning once more.

So brief our existence, a glimpse, at the most,
   Is all we can have of the few we hold dear;
And oft even joy is unheeded and lost,
   For want of some heart, that could echo it, near.
Ah, well may we hope, when this short life is gone,
   To meet in some world of more permanent bliss,
For a smile, or a grasp of the hand, hast'ning on,
   Is all we enjoy of each other in this.

But, come, the more rare such delights to the heart,
   The more we should welcome and bless them the more;
They're ours, when we meet,—they are lost when we part,
   Like birds that bring summer, and fly when 'tis o'er.

Thus circling the cup, hand in hand, ere we drink,
  Let Sympathy pledge us, thro' pleasure, thro' pain,
That, fast as a feeling but touches one link,
  Her magic shall send it direct thro' the chain.

Shall the Harp then be silent.

Shall the Harp then be silent, when he who first gave
    To our country a name, is withdrawn from all eyes?
Shall a Minstrel of Erin stand mute by the grave
    Where the first—where the last of her Patriots lies?

No—faint tho' the death-song may fall from his lips,
    Tho' his Harp, like his soul, may with shadows be crost,
Yet, yet shall it sound, 'mid a nation's eclipse,
    And proclaim to the world what a star hath been lost;[67]—

What a union of all the affections and powers
    By which life is exalted, embellish'd, refined,
Was embraced in that spirit—whose centre was ours,
    While its mighty circumference circled mankind.

D. Maclise, R.A.   F. P. Becker.

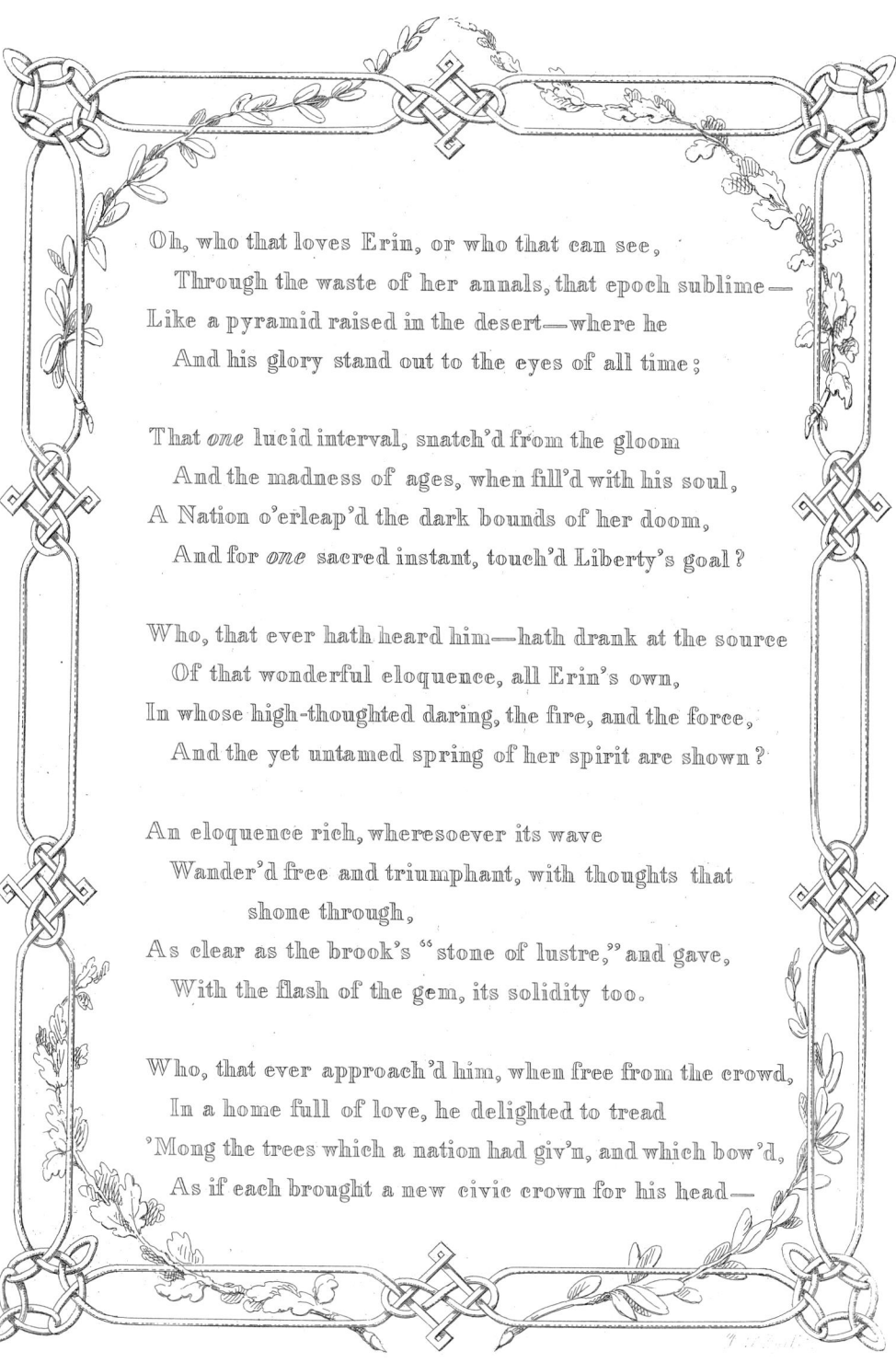

Oh, who that loves Erin, or who that can see,
    Through the waste of her annals, that epoch sublime—
Like a pyramid raised in the desert—where he
    And his glory stand out to the eyes of all time;

That *one* lucid interval, snatch'd from the gloom
    And the madness of ages, when fill'd with his soul,
A Nation o'erleap'd the dark bounds of her doom,
    And for *one* sacred instant, touch'd Liberty's goal?

Who, that ever hath heard him—hath drank at the source
    Of that wonderful eloquence, all Erin's own,
In whose high-thoughted daring, the fire, and the force,
    And the yet untamed spring of her spirit are shown?

An eloquence rich, wheresoever its wave
    Wander'd free and triumphant, with thoughts that shone through,
As clear as the brook's "stone of lustre," and gave,
    With the flash of the gem, its solidity too.

Who, that ever approach'd him, when free from the crowd,
    In a home full of love, he delighted to tread
'Mong the trees which a nation had giv'n, and which bow'd,
    As if each brought a new civic crown for his head—

Is there one, who hath thus, through his orbit of life
    But at distance observed him—through glory, through blame,
In the calm of retreat, in the grandeur of strife,
    Whether shining or clouded, still high and the same,—

Oh no, not a heart, that e'er knew him, but mourns
    Deep, deep o'er the grave, where such glory is shrined—
O'er a monument Fame will preserve, 'mong the urns
    Of the wisest, the bravest, the best of mankind!

Desmond's Song.

By the Feal's wave benighted,
   No star in the skies,
To thy door by Love lighted,
   I first saw those eyes.
Some voice whisper'd o'er me,
   As the threshold I crost,
There was ruin before me,
   If I loved, I was lost.

Love came, and brought sorrow
　Too soon in his train;
Yet so sweet, that to-morrow
　'Twere welcome again.
Though misery's full measure
　My portion should be,
I would drain it with pleasure,
　If pour'd out by thee.

You, who call it dishonour
　To bow to this flame,
If you've eyes, look but on her,
　And blush while you blame.
Hath the pearl less whiteness
　Because of its birth?
Hath the violet less brightness
　For growing near earth?

No—Man for his glory
　To ancestry flies;
But Woman's bright story
　Is told in her eyes.
While the Monarch but traces
　Thro' mortals his line,
Beauty, born of the Graces,
　Ranks next to Divine!

I've a Secret to tell thee.

I've a secret to tell thee, but hush! not here,—
    Oh! not where the world its vigil keeps:
I'll seek, to whisper it in thine ear,
    Some shore where the Spirit of Silence sleeps;
Where summer's wave unmurmuring dies,
    Nor fay can hear the fountain's gush;
Where, if but a note her night-bird sighs,
    The rose saith, chidingly, "Hush, sweet, hush!"

There, amid the deep silence of that hour,
    When stars can be heard in ocean dip,
Thyself shall, under some rosy bower,
    Sit mute, with thy finger on thy lip:
Like him, the boy," who born among
    The flowers that on the Nile-stream blush,
Sits ever thus,—his only song
    To earth and heaven, "Hush, all, hush!"

The Mountain Sprite.

In yonder valley there dwelt, alone,
A youth, whose moments had calmly flown,
Till spells came o'er him, and, day and night,
He was haunted and watch'd by a Mountain Sprite.

As once, by moonlight, he wander'd o'er
The golden sands of that island shore,
A foot-print sparkled before his sight—
'Twas the fairy foot of the Mountain Sprite!

Beside a fountain, one sunny day,
As bending over the stream he lay,
There peep'd down o'er him two eyes of light,
And he saw in that mirror the Mountain Sprite.

He turn'd, but, lo, like a startled bird,
That spirit fled!—and the youth but heard
Sweet music, such as marks the flight
Of some bird of song, from the Mountain Sprite.

One night, still haunted by that bright look,
The boy, bewilder'd, his pencil took,
And, guided only by memory's light,
Drew the once-seen form of the Mountain Sprite.

"Oh thou, who lovest the shadow," cried
A voice, low whispering by his side,
"Now turn and see,"—here the youth's delight
Seal'd the rosy lips of the Mountain Sprite.

"Of all the Spirits of land and sea,"
Then rapt he murmur'd, "there's none like thee,
"And oft, oh oft, may thy foot thus light
"In this lonely bower, sweet Mountain Sprite!"

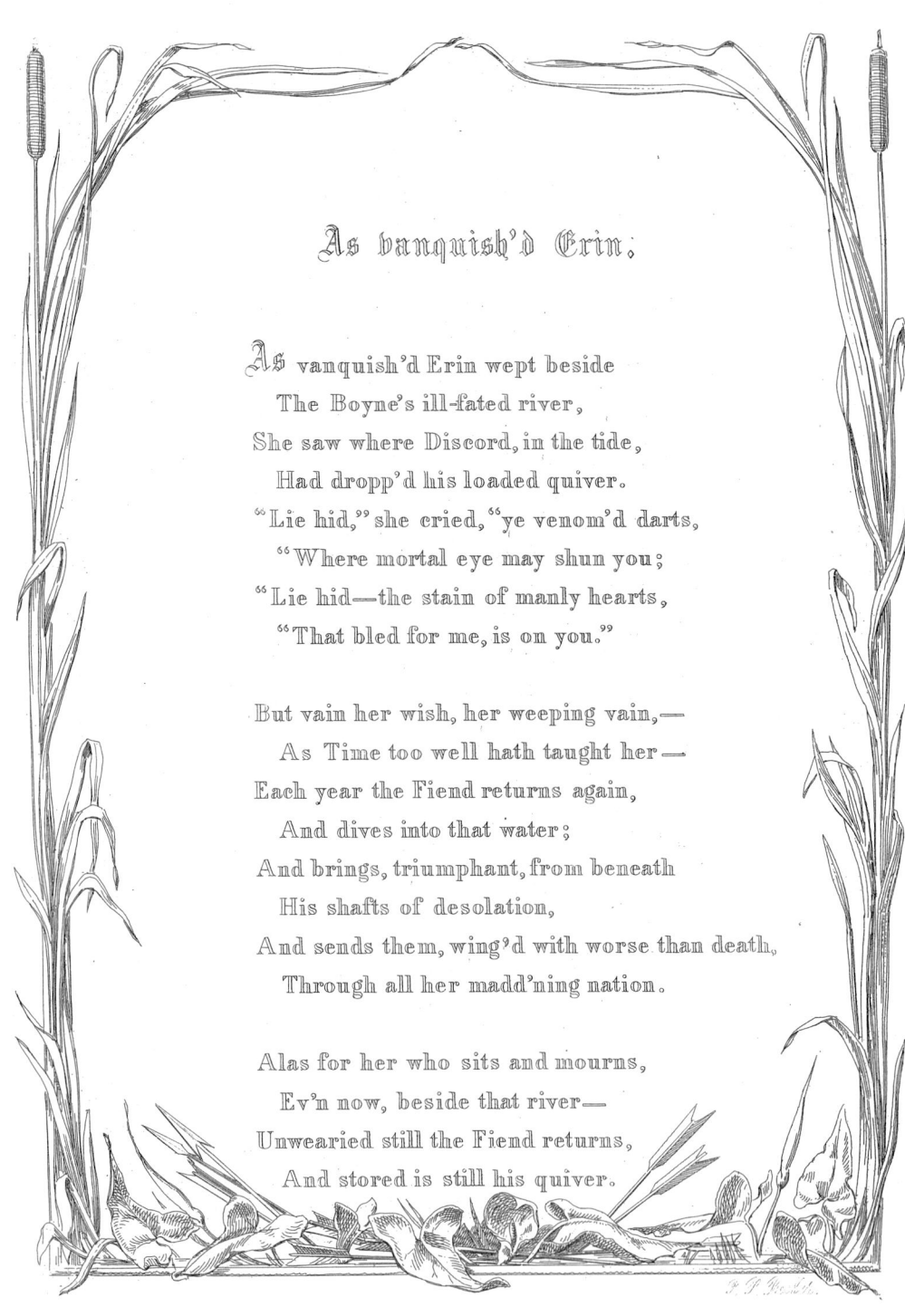

As vanquish'd Erin.

As vanquish'd Erin wept beside
   The Boyne's ill-fated river,
She saw where Discord, in the tide,
   Had dropp'd his loaded quiver.
"Lie hid," she cried, "ye venom'd darts,
   "Where mortal eye may shun you;
"Lie hid—the stain of manly hearts,
   "That bled for me, is on you."

But vain her wish, her weeping vain,—
   As Time too well hath taught her—
Each year the Fiend returns again,
   And dives into that water;
And brings, triumphant, from beneath
   His shafts of desolation,
And sends them, wing'd with worse than death,
   Through all her madd'ning nation.

Alas for her who sits and mourns,
   Ev'n now, beside that river—
Unwearied still the Fiend returns,
   And stored is still his quiver.

"When will this end, ye Powers of Good?"
　　She weeping asks for ever;
But only hears, from out that flood,
　　The Demon answer, "Never!"

Sing, sweet Harp.

Sing, sweet Harp, oh sing to me
　　Some song of ancient days,
Whose sounds, in this sad memory,
　　Long buried dreams shall raise;—
Some lay that tells of vanish'd fame,
　　Whose light once round us shone;
Of noble pride, now turn'd to shame,
　　And hopes for ever gone.—
Sing, sad Harp, thus sing to me;
　　Alike our doom is cast,
Both lost to all but memory,
　　We live but in the past.

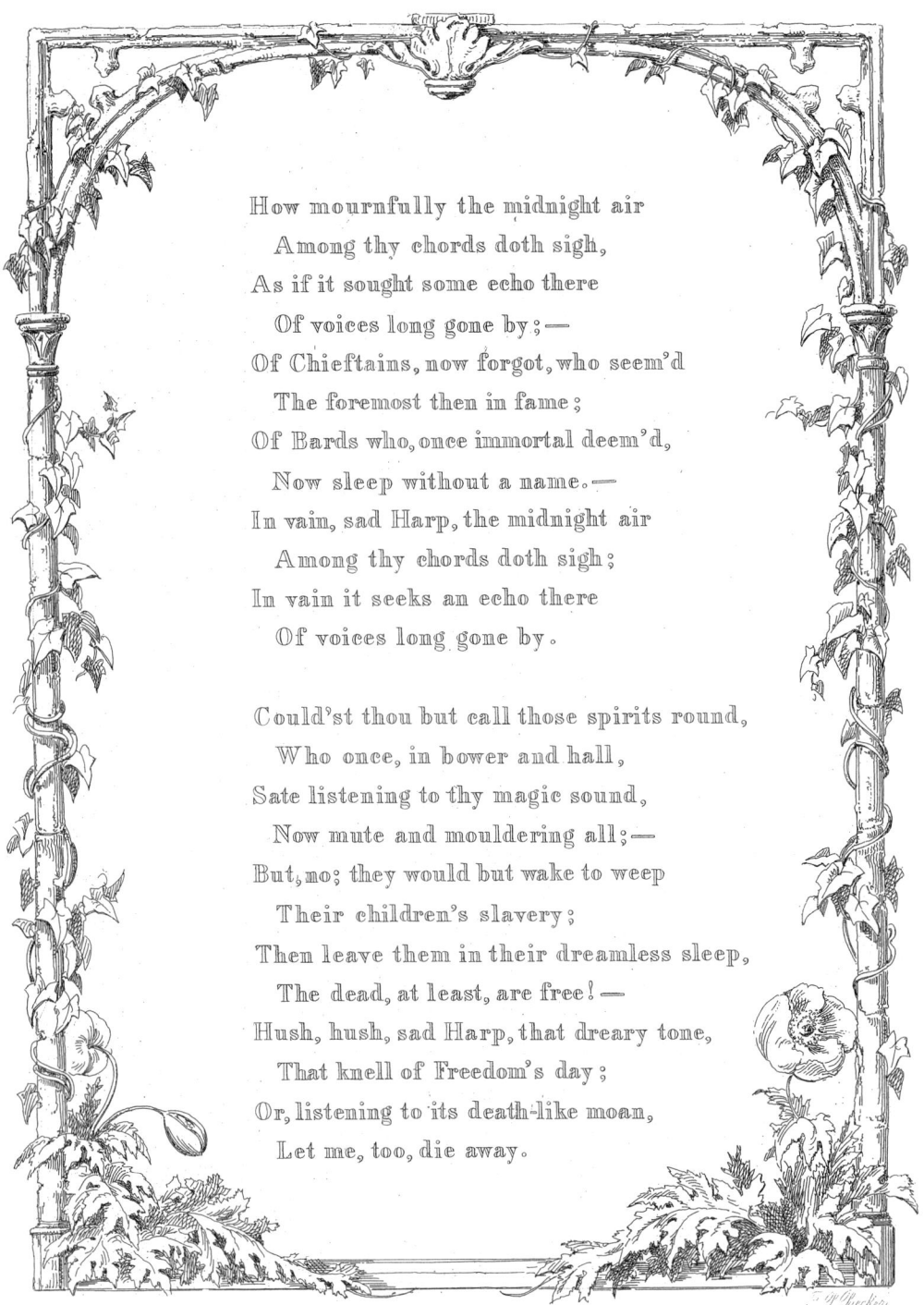

How mournfully the midnight air
  Among thy chords doth sigh,
As if it sought some echo there
  Of voices long gone by;—
Of Chieftains, now forgot, who seem'd
  The foremost then in fame;
Of Bards who, once immortal deem'd,
  Now sleep without a name.—
In vain, sad Harp, the midnight air
  Among thy chords doth sigh;
In vain it seeks an echo there
  Of voices long gone by.

Could'st thou but call those spirits round,
  Who once, in bower and hall,
Sate listening to thy magic sound,
  Now mute and mouldering all;—
But, no; they would but wake to weep
  Their children's slavery;
Then leave them in their dreamless sleep,
  The dead, at least, are free!—
Hush, hush, sad Harp, that dreary tone,
  That knell of Freedom's day;
Or, listening to its death-like moan,
  Let me, too, die away.

She sung of Love.

She sung of Love, while o'er her lyre
   The rosy rays of evening fell,
As if to feed with their soft fire
   The soul within that trembling shell.
The same rich light hung o'er her cheek,
   And play'd around those lips that sung
And spoke, as flowers would sing and speak,
   If Love could lend their leaves a tongue.

But soon the West no longer burn'd,
   Each rosy ray from heav'n withdrew;
And, when to gaze again I turn'd,
   The minstrel's form seem'd fading too.
As if *her* light and heav'n's were one,
   The glory all had left that frame;
And from her glimmering lips the tone,
   As from a parting spirit, came."

Who ever loved, but had the thought
    That he and all he loved must part?
Fill'd with this fear, I flew and caught
    The fading image to my heart—
And cried, "Oh Love! is this thy doom?
"Oh light of youth's resplendent day!
"Must ye then lose your golden bloom,
    "And thus, like sunshine, die away?"

The Night Dance.

Strike the gay harp! see the moon is on high,
    And, as true to her beam as the tides of the ocean,
Young hearts, when they feel the soft light of her eye,
    Obey the mute call, and heave into motion.
Then, sound notes—the gayest, the lightest,
    That ever took wing, when heav'n look'd brightest!
        Again! Again!

Oh! could such heart-stirring music be heard
    In that City of Statues described by romancers,
So wakening its spell, even stone would be stirr'd,
    And statues themselves all start into dancers!

Why then delay, with such sounds in our ears,
    And the flower of Beauty's own garden before us,—
While stars overhead leave the song of their spheres,
    And list'ning to ours, hang wondering o'er us?
Again, that strain!—to hear it thus sounding
    Might set even Death's cold pulses bounding—
        Again! Again!
Oh, what delight when the youthful and gay,
    Each with eye like a sunbeam and foot like a feather,
Thus dance, like the Hours to the music of May,
    And mingle sweet song and sunshine together!

From this Hour the Pledge is given.

From this hour the pledge is given,
   From this hour my soul is thine:
Come what will, from earth or heaven,
   Weal or woe, thy fate be mine.
When the proud and great stood by thee,
   None dared thy rights to spurn;
And if now they're false and fly thee,
   Shall I, too, basely turn?
No;—whate'er the fires that try thee,
   In the same this heart shall burn.

Tho' the sea, where thou embarkest,
   Offers now no friendly shore,
Light may come where all looks darkest,
   Hope hath life, when life seems o'er.
And, of those past ages dreaming,
   When glory deck'd thy brow,
Oft I fondly think, though seeming
   So fall'n and clouded now,
Thou'lt again break forth, all beaming,—
   None so bright, so blest as thou!

"The wine-cup is circling in Almhin's hall,"
And its Chief, 'mid his heroes reclining,
Looks up, with a sigh, to the trophied wall,
Where his sword hangs idly shining.
   When, hark! that shout
   From the vale without,—
"Arm ye quick, the Dane, the Dane is nigh!"
   Ev'ry Chief starts up
   From his foaming cup,
And "To battle, to battle!" is the Finian's cry.

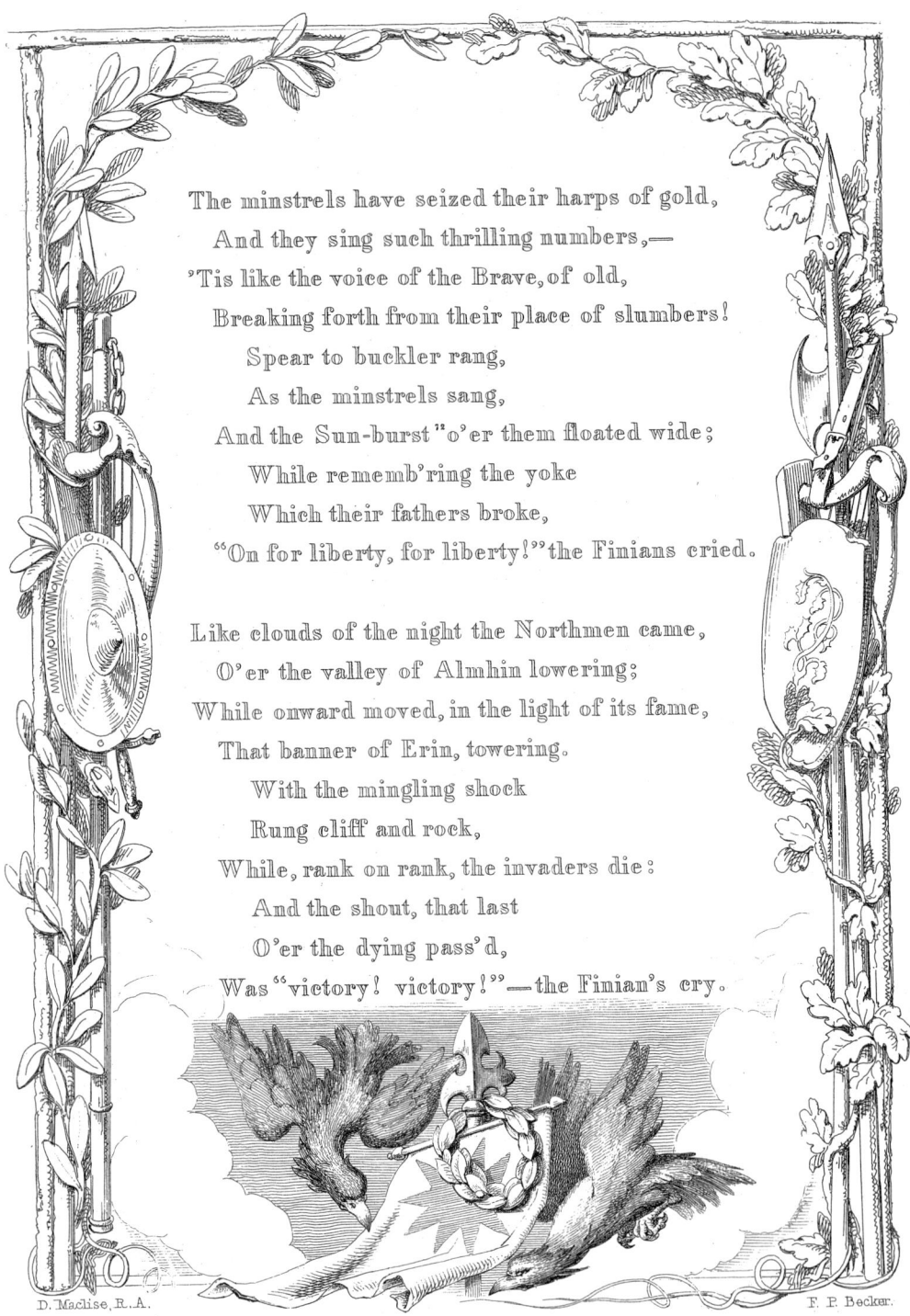

The minstrels have seized their harps of gold,
    And they sing such thrilling numbers,—
'Tis like the voice of the Brave, of old,
    Breaking forth from their place of slumbers!
        Spear to buckler rang,
        As the minstrels sang,
    And the Sun-burst "o'er them floated wide;
        While rememb'ring the yoke
        Which their fathers broke,
"On for liberty, for liberty!" the Finians cried.

Like clouds of the night the Northmen came,
    O'er the valley of Almhin lowering;
While onward moved, in the light of its fame,
    That banner of Erin, towering.
        With the mingling shock
        Rung cliff and rock,
While, rank on rank, the invaders die:
        And the shout, that last
        O'er the dying pass'd,
Was "victory! victory!"—the Finian's cry.

D. Maclise, R. A.   F. P. Becker.

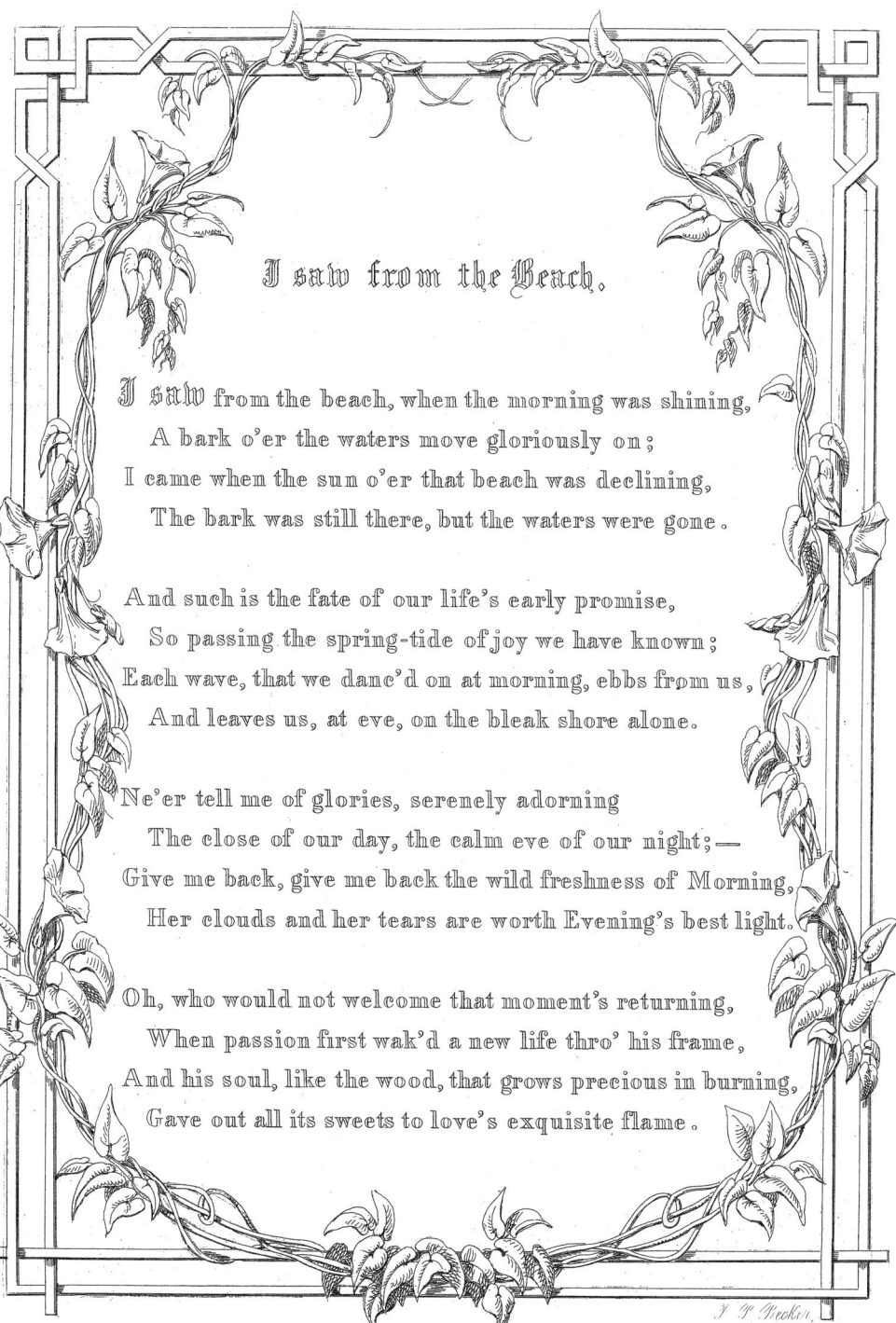

I saw from the Beach.

I saw from the beach, when the morning was shining,
    A bark o'er the waters move gloriously on;
I came when the sun o'er that beach was declining,
    The bark was still there, but the waters were gone.

And such is the fate of our life's early promise,
    So passing the spring-tide of joy we have known;
Each wave, that we danc'd on at morning, ebbs from us,
    And leaves us, at eve, on the bleak shore alone.

Ne'er tell me of glories, serenely adorning
    The close of our day, the calm eve of our night;—
Give me back, give me back the wild freshness of Morning,
    Her clouds and her tears are worth Evening's best light.

Oh, who would not welcome that moment's returning,
    When passion first wak'd a new life thro' his frame,
And his soul, like the wood, that grows precious in burning,
    Gave out all its sweets to love's exquisite flame.

The Dream of those Days.

The dream of those days when first I sung thee is o'er,
Thy triumph hath stain'd the charm thy sorrows then wore;
And ev'n of the light which Hope once shed o'er thy chains,
Alas, not a gleam to grace thy freedom remains.

Say, is it that slavery sunk so deep in thy heart,
That still the dark brand is there, tho' chainless thou art;
And Freedom's sweet fruit, for which thy spirit long burn'd,
Now, reaching at last thy lip, to ashes hath turn'd?

Up Liberty's steep by Truth and Eloquence led,
With eyes on her temple fix'd, how proud was thy tread!
Ah, better thou ne'er had'st lived that summit to gain,
Or died in the porch, than thus dishonour the fane.

Song of the Battle eve.

TIME — THE NINTH CENTURY.

To-morrow, comrade, we
On the battle-plain must be,
   There to conquer, or both lie low!
The morning star is up,—
But there's wine still in the cup,
   And we'll take another quaff, ere we go, boy, go;
   We'll take another quaff, ere we go.

'Tis true, in manliest eyes
A passing tear will rise,
   When we think of the friends we leave lone;
But what can wailing do?
See, our goblet's weeping too!
   With its tears we'll chase away our own, boy,
      our own;
   With its tears we'll chase away our own.

But daylight's stealing on;—
The last that o'er us shone
   Saw our children around us play;
The next—ah! where shall we
And those rosy urchins be?
   But—no matter—grasp thy sword and away,
      boy, away;
   No matter—grasp thy sword and away!

Let those, who brook the chain
Of Saxon or of Dane,
   Ignobly by their fire-sides stay;
One sigh to home be given,
One heartfelt prayer to heaven,
   Then, for Erin and her cause, boy, hurra!
      hurra! hurra!
   Then, for Erin and her cause, hurra!

O'Donohue's Mistress.

Of all the fair months, that round the sun
In light-link'd dance their circles run,
   Sweet May, shine thou for me;
For still, when thy earliest beams arise,
That youth, who beneath the blue lake lies,
   Sweet May, returns to me.

Of all the bright haunts, where daylight leaves
Its lingering smile on golden eves,
   Fair Lake, thou'rt dearest to me;
For when the last April sun grows dim,
Thy Naiads prepare his steed for him [73]
   Who dwells, bright Lake, in thee.

Of all the proud steeds, that ever bore
Young plumed Chiefs on sea or shore,
   White Steed, most joy to thee;
Who still, with the first young glance of spring,
From under that glorious lake dost bring
   My love, my chief, to me.

While, white as the sail some bark unfurls,
When newly launch'd, thy long mane curls,
  Fair Steed, as white and free;
And spirits, from all the lake's deep bowers,
Glide o'er the blue wave scattering flowers,
  Around my love and thee.

Of all the sweet deaths that maidens die,
Whose lovers beneath the cold wave lie,
  Most sweet that death will be,
Which, under the next May evening's light,
When thou and thy steed are lost to sight,
  Dear love, I'll die for thee.

D. Maclise, R.A.   F. Joubert.

The Wandering Bard.

What life like that of the bard can be,—
The wandering bard, who roams as free
As the mountain lark that o'er him sings,
And, like that lark, a music brings
Within him, where'er he comes or goes,—
A fount that for ever flows!
The world's to him like some play-ground,
Where fairies dance their moonlight round;—
If dimm'd the turf where late they trod,
The elves but seek some greener sod;
So, when less bright his scene of glee,
To another away flies he!

Oh, what would have been young Beauty's doom,
Without a bard to fix her bloom?
They tell us, in the moon's bright round,
Things lost in this dark world are found;
So charms, on earth long pass'd and gone,
In the poet's lay live on.—
Would ye have smiles that ne'er grow dim?
You've only to give them all to him,
Who, with but a touch of Fancy's wand,
Can lend them life, this life beyond,
And fix them high, in Poesy's sky,—
Young stars that never die!

Then, welcome the bard where'er he comes,
For, though he hath countless airy homes,
To which his wing excursive roves,
Yet still, from time to time, he loves
To light upon earth and find such cheer
As brightens our banquet here.
No matter how far, how fleet he flies,
You've only to light up kind young eyes,
Such signal-fires as here are given,—
And down he'll drop from Fancy's heaven,
The minute such call to love or mirth
Proclaims he's wanting on earth!

Sing—Sing—Music was given.

Sing — sing—Music was given,
    To brighten the gay, and kindle the loving;
Souls here, like planets in Heaven,
    By harmony's laws alone are kept moving.
Beauty may boast of her eyes and her cheeks,
    But Love from the lips his true archery wings;
And she, who but feathers the dart when she speaks,
    At once sends it home to the heart when she sings.
    Then sing—sing—Music was given,
        To brighten the gay, and kindle the loving;
    Souls here, like planets in Heaven,
        By harmony's laws alone are kept moving.

When Love, rock'd by his mother,
    Lay sleeping as calm as slumber could make him,
"Hush, hush," said Venus, "no other
    "Sweet voice but his own is worthy to wake him."
Dreaming of music he slumber'd the while
    Till faint from his lip a soft melody broke,
And Venus, enchanted, look'd on with a smile,
    While Love to his own sweet singing awoke.
    Then sing—sing—Music was given,
        To brighten the gay, and kindle the loving;
    Souls here, like planets in Heaven,
        By harmony's laws alone are kept moving.

F. P. Becker.

There are sounds of Mirth.

There are sounds of mirth in the night-air ringing,
    And lamps from every casement shown;
While voices blithe within are singing,
    That seem to say "Come," in every tone.
Ah! once how light, in Life's young season,
    My heart had leap'd at that sweet lay;
Nor paus'd to ask of greybeard Reason
    Should I the syren call obey.

And, see—the lamps still livelier glitter,
    The syren lips more fondly sound;
No, seek, ye nymphs, some victim fitter
    To sink in your rosy bondage bound.
Shall a bard, whom not the world in arms
    Could bend to tyranny's rude controul,
Thus quail, at sight of woman's charms,
    And yield to a smile his freeborn soul?

Thus sung the sage, while, slyly stealing,
 The nymphs their fetters around him cast,
And,—their laughing eyes, the while, concealing,—
 Led Freedom's Bard their slave at last.
For the Poet's heart, still prone to loving,
 Was like that rock of the Druid race,[75]
Which the gentlest touch at once set moving,
 But all earth's power couldn't cast from its base.

D. Maclise, R.A.   F. P. Becker.

Song of Innisfail.

They came from a land beyond the sea,
   And now o'er the western main
Set sail, in their good ships, gallantly,
   From the sunny land of Spain.
"Oh, where's the Isle we've seen in dreams,
   "Our destin'd home or grave?"
Thus sung they as, by the morning's beams,
   They swept the Atlantic wave.

And, lo, where afar o'er ocean shines
   A sparkle of radiant green,
As though in that deep lay emerald mines,
   Whose light thro' the wave was seen.
"'Tis Innisfail—'tis Innisfail!"
Rings o'er the echoing sea;
While, bending to heav'n, the warriors hail
   That home of the brave and free.

Then turn'd they unto the Eastern wave,
   Where now their Day-God's eye
A look of such sunny omen gave
   As lighted up sea and sky.

Nor frown was seen through sky or sea,
　Nor tear o'er leaf or sod,
When first on their Isle of Destiny
　Our great forefathers trod.

Alone in Crowds to wander on.

Alone in crowds to wander on,
　And feel that all the charm is gone
Which voices dear and eyes beloved
Shed round us once, where'er we roved—
This, this the doom must be
Of all who've loved, and lived to see
The few bright things they thought would stay
For ever near them, die away.

Tho' fairer forms around us throng,
Their smiles to others all belong,
And want that charm which dwells alone
Round those the fond heart calls its own.

Where, where the sunny brow?
The long-known voice—where are they now?
Thus ask I still, nor ask in vain,
The silence answers all too plain.

Oh, what is Fancy's magic worth,
If all her art cannot call forth
One bliss like those we felt of old
From lips now mute, and eyes now cold?
No, no,—her spell is vain,—
As soon could she bring back again
Those eyes themselves from out the grave,
As wake again one bliss they gave.

Oh! Arranmore, loved Arranmore.

Oh! Arranmore, loved Arranmore,
How oft I dream of thee,
And of those days when, by thy shore,
I wander'd young and free,

Full many a path I've tried, since then,
  Through pleasure's flowery maze,
But ne'er could find the bliss again
  I felt in those sweet days.

How blithe upon thy breezy cliffs
  At sunny morn I've stood,
With heart as bounding as the skiffs
  That danced along thy flood;
Or, when the western wave grew bright
  With daylight's parting wing,
Have sought that Eden in its light
  Which dreaming poets sing;[78]—

That Eden where th'immortal brave
  Dwell in a land serene,—
Whose bowers beyond the shining wave,
  At sunset, oft are seen.
Ah dream too full of sadd'ning truth!
  Those mansions o'er the main
Are like the hopes I built in youth,—
  As sunny and as vain!

Oh, could we do with this World of ours

Oh, could we do with this world of ours
As thou dost with thy garden bowers,
Reject the weeds and keep the flowers,
    What a heaven on earth we'd make it!
So bright a dwelling should be our own,
So warranted free from sigh or frown,
That angels soon would be coming down,
    By the week or month to take it.

Like those gay flies that wing thro' air,
And in themselves a lustre bear,
A stock of light, still ready there,
    Whenever they wish to use it;
So, in this world I'd make for thee,
Our hearts should all like fire-flies be,
And the flash of wit or poesy
    Break forth whenever we choose it.

D. Maclise, R.A.   F. P. Becker.

While ev'ry joy that glads our sphere
Hath still some shadow hovering near,
In this new world of ours, my dear,
 Such shadows will all be omitted:—
Unless they're like that graceful one,
Which, when thou'rt dancing in the sun,
Still near thee, leaves a charm upon
 Each spot where it hath flitted!

"Silence is in our Festal Halls."

Silence is in our festal halls,—
 Sweet Son of Song! thy course is o'er;
In vain on thee sad Erin calls,
 Her minstrel's voice responds no more;—
All silent as th' Eolian shell
 Sleeps at the close of some bright day,
When the sweet breeze, that waked its swell
 At sunny morn, hath died away.

Yet, at our feasts, thy spirit long,
    Awaked by music's spell, shall rise;
For, name so link'd with deathless song
    Partakes its charm and never dies:
And ev'n within the holy fane,
    When music wafts the soul to heaven,
One thought to him, whose earliest strain
    Was echoed there, shall long be given.

But, where is now the cheerful day,
    The social night, when, by thy side,
He, who now weaves this parting lay,
    His skilless voice with thine allied;
And sung those songs whose every tone,
    When bard and minstrel long have past,
Shall still, in sweetness all their own,
    Embalm'd by fame, undying last.

Yes, Erin, thine alone the fame,—
    Or, if thy bard have shared the crown,
From thee the borrow'd glory came,
    And at thy feet is now laid down.
Enough, if Freedom still inspire
    His latest song, and still there be,
As evening closes round his lyre,
    One ray upon its chords from thee.

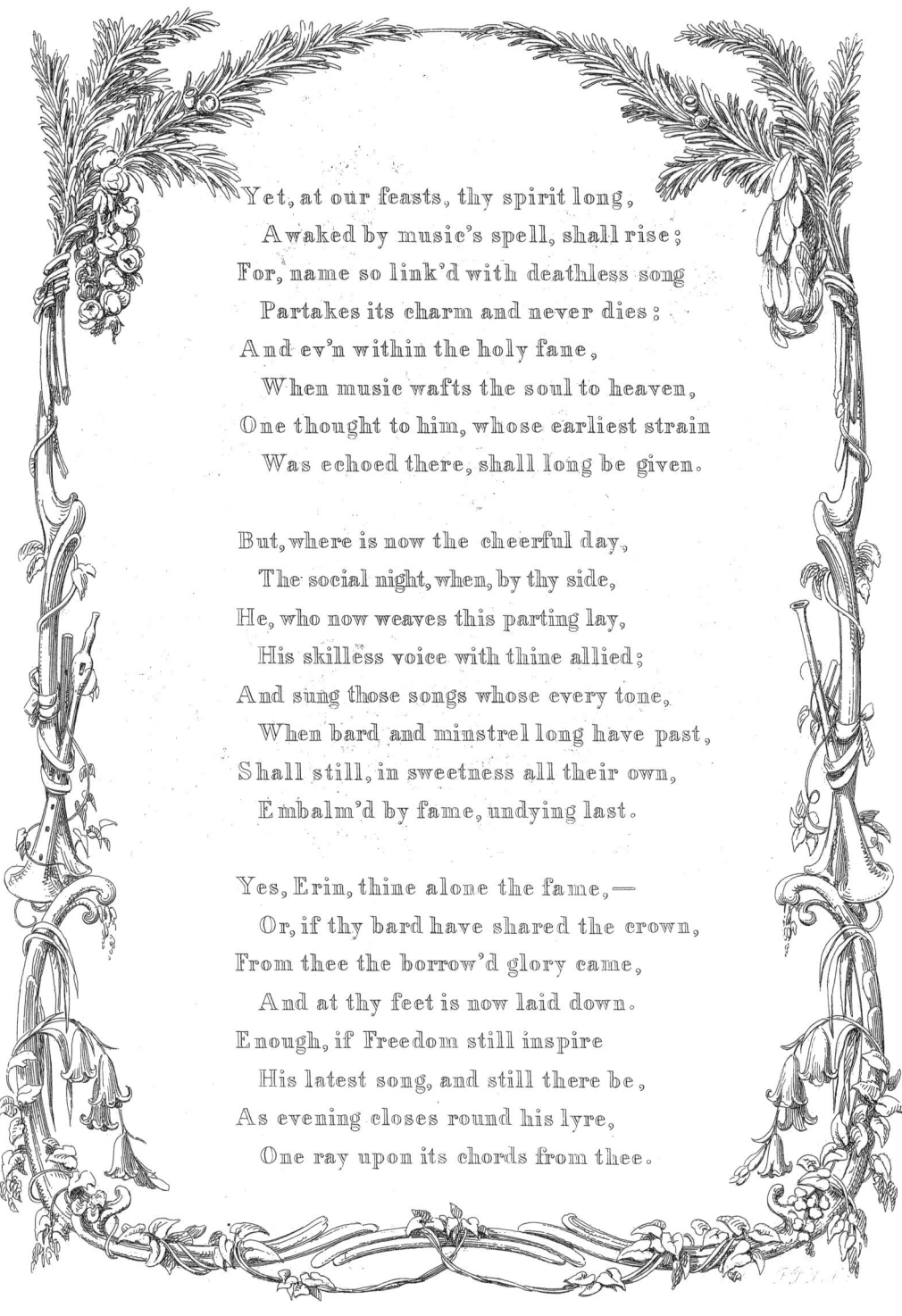

Lay his sword by his side,—it hath served him too well
   Not to rest near his pillow below;
To the last moment true, from his hand ere it fell,
   Its point was still turn'd to a flying foe.
Fellow-lab'rers in life, let them slumber in death,
   Side by side, as becomes the reposing brave,—
That sword which he loved still unbroke in its sheath,
   And himself unsubdued in his grave.

Yet pause—for, in fancy, a still voice I hear,
  As if breathed from his brave heart's remains;—
Faint echo of that which, in Slavery's ear,
  Once sounded the war-word, "Burst your chains!"
And it cries, from the grave where the hero lies deep,
  "Tho' the day of your Chieftain for ever hath set,
"Oh leave not his sword thus inglorious to sleep,—
  "It hath victory's life in it yet!

"Should some alien, unworthy such weapon to wield,
  "Dare to touch thee, my own gallant sword,
"Then rest in thy sheath, like a talisman seal'd,
  "Or return to the grave of thy chainless lord.
"But, if grasp'd by a hand that hath learn'd the proud use
  "Of a falchion, like thee, on the battle-plain,—
"Then, at Liberty's summons, like lightning let loose,
  "Leap forth from thy dark sheath again!"

APPENDIX.

ADVERTISEMENT

PREFIXED TO THE

FIRST AND SECOND NUMBERS.

Though the beauties of the National Music of Ireland have been very generally felt and acknowledged, yet it has happened, through the want of appropriate English words, and of the arrangement necessary to adapt them to the voice, that many of the most excellent compositions have hitherto remained in obscurity. It is intended, therefore, to form a Collection of the best Original Irish Melodies, with characteristic Symphonies and Accompaniments; and with Words containing, as frequently as possible, allusions to the manners and history of the country. Sir John Stevenson has very kindly consented to undertake the arrangement of the Airs; and the lovers of Simple National Music may rest secure, that in such tasteful hands, the native charms of the original melody will not be sacrificed to the ostentation of science.

PREFATORY NOTICES.

In the poetical Part, promises of assistance have been received from several distinguished Literary Characters; particularly from Mr. MOORE, whose lyrical talent is so peculiarly suited to such a task, and whose zeal in the undertaking will be best understood from the following Extract of a Letter which he has addressed to Sir JOHN STEVENSON on the subject : —

I feel very anxious that a work of this kind should be undertaken. We have too long neglected the only talent for which our English neighbours ever deigned to allow us any credit. Our National Music has never been properly collected[*]; and, while the composers of the Continent have enriched their Operas and Sonatas with Melodies borrowed from Ireland — very often without even the honesty of acknowledgment — we have left these treasures, in a great degree, unclaimed and fugitive. Thus our Airs, like too many of our countrymen, have, for want of protection at home, passed into the service of foreigners. But we are come, I hope, to a better period

---

[*] The writer forgot, when he made this assertion, that the public are indebted to Mr. BUNTING for a very valuable collection of Irish Music; and that the patriotic genius of Miss OWENSON has been employed upon some of our finest airs.

PREFATORY NOTICES.

of both Politics and Music; and how much they are connected, in Ireland at least, appears too plainly in the tone of sorrow and depression which characterises most of our early Songs.

The task which you propose to me, of adapting words to these airs, is by no means easy. The Poet, who would follow the various sentiments which they express, must feel and understand that rapid fluctuation of spirits, that unaccountable mixture of gloom and levity, which composes the character of my countrymen, and has deeply tinged their Music. Even in their liveliest strains we find some melancholy note intrude,—some minor Third or flat Seventh,—which throws its shade as it passes, and makes even mirth interesting. If BURNS had been an Irishman (and I would willingly give up all our claims upon OSSIAN for him), his heart would have been proud of such music, and his genius would have made it immortal.

Another difficulty (which is, however, purely mechanical) arises from the irregular structure of many of those airs, and the lawless kind of metre which it will in consequence be necessary to adapt to them. In these instances the Poet must write, not to the eye, but to the ear; and must be content to have his verses of that description which CICERO mentions, "*Quos si cantu spo-*

PREFATORY NOTICES.

liaveris nuda remanebit oratio." That beautiful Air, "The Twisting of the Rope," which has all the romantic character of the Swiss *Ranz des Vaches*, is one of those wild and sentimental rakes which it will not be very easy to tie down in sober wedlock with Poetry. However, notwithstanding all these difficulties, and the very little talent which I can bring to surmount them, the design appears to me so truly National, that I shall feel much pleasure in giving it all the assistance in my power.

Leicestershire, Feb. 1807.

ADVERTISEMENT

TO THE

THIRD NUMBER.

In presenting the Third Number of this work to the Public, the Publisher begs leave to offer his acknowledgments for the very liberal patronage with which it has been honoured; and to express a hope that the unabated zeal of those who have hitherto so admirably conducted it, will enable him to continue it through many future Numbers with equal spirit, variety, and taste. The stock of popular Melodies is far from being exhausted; and there is still in reserve an abundance of beautiful Airs, which call upon Mr. MOORE, in the language he so well understands, to save them from the oblivion to which they are hastening.

LETTER ON MUSIC,

TO

THE MARCHIONESS DOWAGER OF DONEGAL.

PREFIXED TO THE THIRD NUMBER.

WHILE the Publisher of these Melodies very properly inscribes them to the Nobility and Gentry of Ireland in general, I have much pleasure in selecting *one* from that number, to whom *my* share of the work is particularly dedicated. Though your Ladyship has been so long absent from Ireland, I know that you remember it well

LETTER ON MUSIC.

and warmly — that you have not allowed the charm of English society, like the taste of the lotus, to produce oblivion of your country, but that even the humble tribute which I offer derives its chief claim upon your interest from the appeal which it makes to your patriotism. Indeed, absence, however fatal to some affections of the heart, rather strengthens our love for the land where we were born; and Ireland is the country, of all others, which an exile from it must remember with most enthusiasm. Those few darker and less amiable traits with which bigotry and misrule have stained her character, and which are too apt to disgust us upon a nearer intercourse, become softened at a distance, or altogether invisible; and nothing is remembered but her virtues and her misfortunes — the zeal with which she has always loved liberty, and the barbarous policy which has always withheld it from her — the ease with which her generous spirit might be conciliated, and the cruel ingenuity which has been exerted to " wring her into undutifulness." *

It has been often remarked, and oftener felt, that our music is the truest of all comments upon our history.

---

* A phrase which occurs in a Letter from the Earl of Desmond to the Earl of Ormond, in Elizabeth's time, — *Scrinia Sacra*, as quoted by Curry.

LETTER ON MUSIC.

The tone of defiance, succeeded by the languor of despondency — a burst of turbulence dying away into softness — the sorrows of one moment lost in the levity of the next — and all that romantic mixture of mirth and sadness, which is naturally produced by the efforts of a lively temperament to shake off, or forget, the wrongs which lie upon it, — such are the features of our history and character, which we find strongly and faithfully reflected in our music; and there are even many airs, which it is difficult to listen to, without recalling some period or event to which their expression seems applicable. Sometimes, when the strain is open and spirited, yet shaded here and there by a mournful recollection, we can fancy that we behold the brave allies of Montrose*, marching to the aid of the royal cause, notwithstanding all the perfidy of Charles and his ministers, and remembering just enough of past sufferings to enhance the generosity of their present sacrifice. The plaintive melodies of

---

* There are some gratifying accounts of the gallantry of these Irish auxiliaries in "The Complete History of the Wars in Scotland under Montrose" (1660). See particularly, for the conduct of an Irishman at the battle of Aberdeen, chap. vi. p. 49.; and for a tribute to the bravery of Colonel O'Kyan, chap. vii. 55. Clarendon owns that the Marquis of Montrose was indebted for much of his miraculous success to the small band of Irish heroes under Macdonnell.

LETTER ON MUSIC.

Carolan take us back to the times in which he lived, when our poor countrymen were driven to worship their God in caves, or to quit for ever the land of their birth — like the bird that abandons the nest which human touch has violated; and in many a song do we hear the last farewell of the exile*, mingling sad regret for the ties he leaves at home, with sanguine expectations of the honours that await him abroad — such honours as were won on the field of Fontenoy, where the valour of Irish Catholics turned the fortune of the day, and extorted from George the Second that memorable exclamation, " Cursed be the laws which deprive me of such subjects!"

Though much has been said of the antiquity of our music, it is certain that our finest and most popular airs

---

* The associations of the Hindu music, though more obvious and defined, were far less touching and characteristic. They divided their songs according to the seasons of the year, by which (says Sir William Jones) "they were able to recall the memory of autumnal merriment, at the close of the harvest, or of separation and melancholy during the cold months," &c. — *Asiatic Transactions*, vol. iii., on the Musical Modes of the Hindus. — What the Abbé du Bos says of the symphonies of Lully, may be asserted, with much more probability of our bold and impassioned airs — "elles auroient produit de ces effets, qui nous paroissent fabuleux dans le récit des anciens, si on les avoit fait entendre à des hommes d'un naturel aussi vif que les Athéniens."— *Reflex. sur la Peinture, &c.* tom. i. sect. 45.

LETTER ON MUSIC.

are modern; and perhaps we may look no further than the last disgraceful century for the origin of most of those wild and melancholy strains, which were at once the offspring and solace of grief, and were applied to the mind as music was formerly to the body, "decantare loca dolentia." Mr. Pinkerton is of opinion* that none of the Scotch popular airs are as old as the middle of the sixteenth century; and though musical antiquaries refer us, for some of our melodies, to so early a period as the fifth century, I am persuaded that there are few, of a *civilized* description (and by this I mean to exclude all the savage Ceanans, Cries†, &c.), which can claim quite so ancient a date as Mr. Pinkerton allows to the Scotch. But music is not the only subject upon which our taste for antiquity is rather unreasonably indulged; and, however heretical it may be to dissent from these romantic speculations, I cannot help thinking that it is possible to love our country very zealously, and to feel deeply interested in her honour and happiness, without believing that Irish was the language spoken in Paradise‡; that our ancestors were kind

---

* Dissertation, prefixed to the 2d volume of his Scottish Ballads.

† Of which some genuine specimens may be found at the end of Mr. Walker's Work upon the Irish bards. Mr. Bunting has disfigured his last splendid volume by too many of these barbarous rhapsodies.

‡ See Advertisement to the Transactions of the Gaelic Society of Dublin.

LETTER ON MUSIC.

enough to take the trouble of polishing the Greeks*, or that Abaris, the Hyperborean, was a native of the North of Ireland.†

By some of these archæologists it has been imagined that the Irish were early acquainted with counter-point‡; and they endeavour to support this conjecture by a well-known passage in Giraldus, where he dilates, with such elaborate praise, upon the beauties of our national minstrelsy. But the terms of this eulogy are too vague, too deficient in technical accuracy, to prove that even Giraldus himself knew any thing of the artifice of counter-point. There are many expressions in the Greek and Latin writers which might be cited, with much more plausibility, to prove that they understood the arrangement of music in

* O'Halloran, vol. i. part iv. chap. vii.
† Id. ib. chap. vi.

‡ It is also supposed, but with as little proof, that they understood the diésis, or enharmonic interval. — The Greeks seem to have formed their ears to this delicate gradation of sound; and, whatever difficulties or objections may lie in the way of its practical use, we must agree with Mersenne (Préludes de l'Harmonie, quest. 7.), that the theory of Music would be imperfect without it; and even in practice (as Tosi, among others, very justly remarks, Observations on Florid Song, chap. i. sect. 16.), there is no good performer on the violin who does not make a sensible difference between D sharp and E flat, though, from the imperfection of the instrument, they are the same notes upon the piano-forte. The effect of modulation by enharmonic transitions is also very striking and beautiful.

parts*; yet I believe it is conceded in general by the learned, that, however grand and pathetic the melody of the ancients may have been, it was reserved for the ingenuity of modern Science to transmit the "light of Song" through the variegating prism of Harmony.

Indeed, the irregular scale of the early Irish (in which, as in the music of Scotland, the interval of the fourth was wanting†,) must have furnished but wild and refractory subjects to the harmonist. It was only when the invention

---

* The words ποικιλια and ἑτεροφωνια, in a passage of Plato, and some expressions of Cicero in Fragment., lib. ii. de Republ., induced the Abbé Fraguier to maintain that the ancients had a knowledge of counterpoint. M. Burette, however, has answered him, I think, satisfactorily. (Examen d'un Passage de Platon, in the 3d vol. of Histoire de l'Acad.) M. Huet is of opinion (Pensées Diverses), that what Cicero says of the music of the spheres, in his dream of Scipio, is sufficient to prove an acquaintance with harmony; but one of the strongest passages, which I recollect, in favour of the supposition, occurs in the Treatise attributed to Aristotle — Περι Κοσμου, Μουσικη δε οξεις ἁμα και βαρεις, κ. τ. λ.

† Another lawless peculiarity of our music is the frequency of what composers call, consecutive fifths; but this is an irregularity which can hardly be avoided by persons not very conversant with the rules of composition; indeed, if I may venture to cite my own wild attempts in this way, it is a fault which I find myself continually committing, and which has sometimes appeared so pleasing to my ear, that I have surrendered it to the critic with no small reluctance. May there not be a little pedantry in adhering too rigidly to this rule? — I have been told that there are instances in Haydn, of an undisguised succession of fifths; and Mr. Shield, in his Introduction to Harmony, seems to intimate that Handel has been sometimes guilty of the same irregularity.

LETTER ON MUSIC.

of Guido began to be known, and the powers of the harp* were enlarged by additional strings, that our melodies took the sweet character which interests us at present; and while the Scotch persevered in the old mutilation of the scale†, our music became gradually more amenable to the laws of harmony and counter-point.

* A singular oversight occurs in an Essay upon the Irish Harp, by Mr. Beauford, which is inserted in the Appendix to Walker's Historical Memoirs: — " The Irish (says he) according to Bromton, in the reign of Henry II. had two kinds of Harps, 'Hibernici tamen in duobus musici generis instrumentis, quamvis præcipitem et velocem, suavem tamen et jucundum :' the one greatly bold and quick, the other soft and pleasing." — How a man of Mr. Beauford's learning could so mistake the meaning, and mutilate the grammatical construction of this extract, is unaccountable. The following is the passage as I find it entire in Bromton; and it requires but little Latin to perceive the injustice which has been done to the words of the old Chronicler: — " Et cum Scotia, hujus terræ filia, utatur lyrâ, tympano et choro, ac Wallia cithara, tubis et choro Hibernici tamen in duobus musici generis instrumentis, *quamvis præcipitem et velocem, suavem tamen et jucundam,* crispatis modulis et intricatis notulis, *efficiunt harmoniam.*" — Hist. Anglic. Script. page 1075. I should not have thought this error worth remarking, but that the compiler of the Dissertation on the Harp, prefixed to Mr. Bunting's last Work, has adopted it implicitly.

† The Scotch lay claim to some of our best airs, but there are strong traits of difference between their melodies and ours. They had formerly the same passion for robbing us of our Saints, and the learned Dempster was for this offence called " The Saint Stealer." It was an Irishman, I suppose, who, by way of reprisal, stole Dempster's beautiful wife from him at Pisa.—See this anecdote in the *Pinacotheca* of Erythræus, part i. p. 25.

LETTER ON MUSIC.

In profiting, however, by the improvements of the moderns, our style still keeps its originality sacred from their refinements; and though Carolan had frequent opportunities of hearing the works of Germiniani and other masters, we but rarely find him sacrificing his native simplicity to the ambition of their ornaments, or affectation of their science. In that curious composition, indeed, called his Concerto, it is evident that he laboured to imitate Corelli; and this union of manners, so very dissimilar, produces the same kind of uneasy sensation which is felt at a mixture of different styles of architecture. In general, however, the artless flow of our music has preserved itself free from all tinge of foreign innovation*, and the chief corruptions of which we have to complain arise from the unskilful performance of our own itinerant musicians, from whom, too frequently, the airs are noted down, en-

---

* Among other false refinements of the art, our music (with the exception perhaps of the air called " Mamma, Mamma," and one or two more of the same ludicrous description,) has avoided that puerile mimicry of natural noises, motions, &c., which disgraces so often the works of even Handel himself. D'Alembert ought to have had better taste than to become the patron of this imitative affectation. — *Discours Préliminaire de l'Encyclopédie.* The reader may find some good remarks on the subject in Avison upon Musical Expression; a work which, though under the name of Avison, was written, it is said, by Dr. Brown.

cumbered by their tasteless decorations, and responsible for all their ignorant anomalies. Though it be sometimes impossible to trace the original strain, yet, in most of them, "auri per ramos *aura* refulget*," the pure gold of the melody shines through the ungraceful foliage which surrounds it—and the most delicate and difficult duty of a compiler is to endeavour, as much as possible, by retrenching these inelegant superfluities, and collating the various methods of playing or singing each air, to restore the regularity of its form, and the chaste simplicity of its character.

I must again observe, that in doubting the antiquity of our music, my scepticism extends but to those polished specimens of the art, which it is difficult to conceive anterior to the dawn of modern improvement; and that I would by no means invalidate the claims of Ireland to as early a rank in the annals of minstrelsy, as the most zealous antiquary may be inclined to allow her. In addition, indeed, to the power which music must always have possessed over the minds of a people so ardent and susceptible, the stimulus of persecution was not wanting to quicken our taste into enthusiasm; the charms of song

---

* Virgil, Æneid, lib. vi. verse 204.

were ennobled with the glories of martyrdom, and the acts against minstrels, in the reigns of Henry VIII. and Elizabeth, were as successful, I doubt not, in making my countrymen musicians, as the penal laws have been in keeping them Catholics.

With respect to the verses which I have written for these Melodies, as they are intended rather to be sung than read, I can answer for their sound with somewhat more confidence than for their sense. Yet it would be affectation to deny that I have given much attention to the task, and that it is not through want of zeal or industry, if I unfortunately disgrace the sweet airs of my country, by poetry altogether unworthy of their taste, their energy, and their tenderness.

Though the humble nature of my contributions to this work may exempt them from the rigours of literary criticism, it was not to be expected that those touches of political feeling, those tones of national complaint, in which the poetry sometimes sympathizes with the music, would be suffered to pass without censure or alarm. It has been accordingly said, that the tendency of this publication is mischievous*, and that I have chosen these airs but as

---

* See Letters, under the signatures of Timæus, &c., in the *Morning Post, Pilot,* and other papers.

LETTER ON MUSIC.

a vehicle of dangerous politics — as fair and precious vessels (to borrow an image of St. Augustin*), from which the wine of error might be administered. To those who identify nationality with treason, and who see, in every effort for Ireland, a system of hostility towards England, — to those, too, who, nursed in the gloom of prejudice, are alarmed by the faintest gleam of liberality that threatens to disturb their darkness — like that Demophon of old, who, when the sun shone upon him, shivered† — to such men I shall not deign to offer an apology for the warmth of any political sentiment which may occur in the course of these pages. But as there are many, among the more wise and tolerant, who, with feeling enough to mourn over the wrongs of their country, and sense enough to perceive all the danger of not redressing them, may yet think that allusions in the least degree bold or inflammatory should be avoided in a publication of this popular description — I beg of these respected persons to believe, that there is no one who deprecates more sincerely than I do, any appeal to the passions of an ignorant and angry

---

* "Non accuso verba, quasi vasa electa atque pretiosa; sed vinum erroris quod cum eis nobis propinatur." — Lib. i. Confess. chap. 16.

† This emblem of modern bigots was head-butler (τραπεζοποιος) to Alexander the Great. — *Sext. Empir. Pyrrh. Hypoth.* lib. i.

LETTER ON MUSIC.

multitude; but that it is not through that gross and inflammable region of society a work of this nature could ever have been intended to circulate. It looks much higher for its audience and readers: it is found upon the piano-fortes of the rich and the educated — of those who can afford to have their national zeal a little stimulated, without exciting much dread of the excesses into which it may hurry them; and of many whose nerves may be, now and then, alarmed with advantage, as much more is to be gained by their fears than could ever be expected from their justice.

Having thus adverted to the principal objection which has been hitherto made to the poetical part of this work, allow me to add a few words in defence of my ingenious coadjutor, Sir John Stevenson, who has been accused of having spoiled the simplicity of the airs by the chromatic richness of his symphonies, and the elaborate variety of his harmonies. We might cite the example of the admirable Haydn, who has sported through all the mazes of musical science, in his arrangement of the simplest Scottish melodies; but it appears to me, that Sir John Stevenson has brought a national feeling to this task, which it would be in vain to expect from a foreigner, however tasteful or judicious. Through many of his own compositions we trace a vein of Irish sentiment, which points him out as peculiarly suited to catch the spirit of his country's music; and, far from agreeing with those fastidious critics who think that his symphonies have nothing kindred with the airs which they introduce, I would say that, in general, they resemble those illuminated initials of old manuscripts, which are of the same character with the writing which follows, though more highly coloured and more curiously ornamented.

In those airs, which are arranged for voices, his skill has particularly distinguished itself; and, though it cannot be denied that a single melody most naturally expresses the language of feeling and passion, yet often, when a favourite strain has been dismissed, as having lost its charm of novelty for the year, it returns, in a harmonised shape, with new claims upon our interest and attention; and to those who study the delicate artifices of composition, the construction of the inner parts of these pieces must afford, I think, considerable satisfaction. Every voice has an air to itself, a flowing succession of notes, which might be heard with pleasure, independently of the rest — so artfully has the harmonist (if I may thus express it) *gavelled* the melody, distributing an equal portion of its sweetness to every part.

LETTER ON MUSIC.

If your Ladyship's love of Music were not known to me, I should not have hazarded so long a letter upon the subject; but as, probably, I may have presumed too far upon your partiality, the best revenge you can take is to write me just as long a letter upon Painting; and I promise to attend to your theory of the art, with a pleasure only surpassed by that which I have so often derived from your practice of it. — May the mind which such talents adorn continue calm as it is bright, and happy as it is virtuous!

Believe me, your Ladyship's
Grateful Friend and Servant,
THOMAS MOORE.

ADVERTISEMENT

TO THE

FOURTH NUMBER.

THIS Number of the MELODIES ought to have appeared much earlier; and the writer of the words is ashamed to confess, that the delay of its publication must be imputed chiefly, if not entirely, to him. He finds it necessary to

PREFATORY NOTICES.

make this avowal, not only for the purpose of removing all blame from the Publisher, but in consequence of a rumour which has been circulated industriously in Dublin, that the Irish Government had interfered to prevent the continuance of the Work.

This would be, indeed, a revival of HENRY the EIGHTH's enactments against Minstrels, and it is flattering to find that so much importance is attached to our compilation, even by such persons as the inventors of the report. Bishop LOWTH, it is true, was of opinion, that *one* song, like the *Hymn* to *Harmodius*, would have done more towards rousing the spirit of the Romans than *all* the Philippics of CICERO. But we live in wiser and less musical times: ballads have long lost their revolutionary powers; and we question if even a "Lillibullero" would produce any very *serious* consequences at present. It is needless, therefore, to add, that there is no truth in the report; and we trust that whatever belief it obtained was founded rather upon the character of *the Government* than of *the Work*.

The Airs of the last Number, though full of originality and beauty, were, perhaps, in general, too curiously selected to become all at once as popular as, we think, they deserve to be. The Public are remarkably reserved

PREFATORY NOTICES.

towards new acquaintances in music, which, perhaps, is one of the reasons why many modern composers introduce none but old friends to their notice. Indeed, it is natural that persons, who love music only by association, should be slow in feeling the charms of a new and strange melody; while those, who have a quick sensibility for this enchanting art, will as naturally seek and enjoy novelty, because in every variety of strain they find a fresh combination of ideas; and the sound has scarcely reached the ear, before the heart has rapidly translated it into sentiment. After all, however, it cannot be denied that the most popular of our National Airs are also the most beautiful; and it has been our wish in the present Number, to select from those Melodies only which have long been listened to and admired. The least known in the collection is the Air of " *Love's Young Dream ;*" but it is one of those easy, artless strangers, whose merit the heart acknowledges instantly.

T. M.

Bury Street, St. James's,
   Nov. 1811.

PREFATORY NOTICES.

ADVERTISEMENT

TO THE

FIFTH NUMBER.

It is but fair to those, who take an interest in this Work, to state that it is now very near its termination, and that the Sixth Number, which shall speedily appear, will, most probably, be the last of the series. Three volumes will then have been completed, according to the original plan, and the Proprietors desire me to say that a List of Subscribers will be published with the concluding Number.

It is not so much from a want of materials, and still less from any abatement of zeal or industry, that we have adopted the resolution of bringing our task to a close; but we feel so proud, for our country's sake and our own, of the interest which this purely Irish Work has excited, and so anxious lest a particle of that interest should be lost by any ill-judged protraction of its existence, that we think it wiser to take away the cup from the lip, while its flavour is yet, we trust, fresh and sweet, than to risk

PREFATORY NOTICES.

any longer trial of the charm, or give so much as not to leave some wish for more. In speaking thus, I allude entirely to the Airs, which are, of course, the main attraction of these Volumes; and though we have still many popular and delightful Melodies to produce*, yet it cannot be denied that we should soon experience some difficulty in equalling the richness and novelty of the earlier numbers, for which, as we had the choice of all before us, we naturally selected only the most rare and beautiful. The Poetry, too, would be sure to sympathise with the decline of the Music; and, however feebly my words have kept pace with the *excellence* of the Airs, they would follow their *falling off*, I fear, with wonderful alacrity. So that, altogether, both pride and prudence counsel us to stop, while the Work is yet, we believe, flourishing and attractive, and in the imperial attitude " *stantes mori*," before we incur the charge either of altering for the worse, or what is equally unpardonable, continuing too long the same.

* Among these is *Savourna Deelish*, which I have hitherto only withheld from the diffidence I feel in treading upon the same ground with Mr. Campbell, whose beautiful words to this fine Air have taken too strong possession of all ears and hearts, for me to think of producing any impression after him. I suppose, however, I must attempt it for the next Number.

PREFATORY NOTICES.

We beg, however, to say, it is only in the event of our failing to find Airs as exquisite as most of those we have given, that we mean thus to anticipate the natural period of dissolution—like those Indians who put their relatives to death when they become feeble—and they who wish to retard this Euthanasia of the Irish Melodies, cannot better effect it than by contributing to our collection, not what are called curious Airs, for we have abundance of them, and they are, in general, *only* curious, but any real sweet and expressive Songs of our Country, which either chance or research may have brought into their hands.

T. M.

Mayfield Cottage, Ashbourne,
   December, 1813.

ADVERTISEMENT

TO THE

SIXTH NUMBER.

In presenting this Sixth Number to the Public as our last, and bidding adieu to the Irish Harp for ever, we shall not answer very confidently for the strength of our resolution, nor feel quite sure that it may not prove, after all, to be

PREFATORY NOTICES.

only one of those eternal farewells which a lover takes of his mistress occasionally. Our only motive, indeed, for discontinuing the Work was a fear that our treasures were nearly exhausted, and an unwillingness to descend to the gathering of mere seed-pearl, after the very valuable gems it has been our lot to string together. The announcement, however, of this intention, in our Fifth Number, has excited a degree of anxiety in the lovers of Irish Music, not only pleasant and flattering, but highly useful to us; for the various contributions we have received in consequence have enriched our collection with so many choice and beautiful Airs, that if we keep to our resolution of publishing no more, it will certainly be an instance of forbearance and self-command, unexampled in the history of poets and musicians. To one Gentleman in particular, who has been many years resident in England, but who has not forgot, among his various pursuits, either the language or the melodies of his native country, we beg to offer our best thanks for the many interesting communications with which he has favoured us; and we trust that he and our other friends will not relax in those efforts by which we have been so considerably assisted; for, though the work must now be considered as defunct, yet — as Reaumur, the naturalist,

PREFATORY NOTICES.

found out the art of making the cicada sing after it was dead—it is not impossible that, some time or other, we may try a similar experiment upon the Irish Melodies.

T. M.

Mayfield Ashbourne,
  March, 1815.

ADVERTISEMENT

TO THE

SEVENTH NUMBER.

IF I had consulted only my own judgment, this Work would not have extended beyond the Six Numbers already published; which contain, perhaps, the flower of our national melodies, and have attained a rank in public favour, of which I would not willingly risk the forfeiture, by degenerating, in any way, from those merits that were its source. Whatever treasures of our music were still in reserve, (and it will be seen, I trust, that they are numerous and valuable,) I would gladly have left to future poets to glean, and, with the ritual words "*tibi trado,*"

PREFATORY NOTICES.

would have delivered up the torch into other hands, before it had lost much of its light in my own. But the call for a continuance of the work has been, as I understand from the Publisher, so general, and we have received so many contributions of old and beautiful airs*, the suppression of which, for the enhancement of those we have published, would resemble too much the policy of the Dutch in burning their spices, that I have been persuaded, though not without considerable diffidence in my success, to commence a new series of the Irish Melodies.

T. M.

---

* One Gentleman, in particular, whose name I shall feel happy in being allowed to mention, has not only sent us nearly forty ancient airs, but has communicated many curious fragments of Irish poetry, and some interesting traditions current in the country where he resides, illustrated by sketches of the romantic scenery to which they refer; all of which, though too late for the present Number, will be of infinite service to us in the prosecution of our task.

PREFATORY NOTICES.

DEDICATION

TO

THE MARCHIONESS OF HEADFORT,

PREFIXED TO THE

TENTH NUMBER.

It is with a pleasure, not unmixed with melancholy, that I dedicate the last Number of the Irish Melodies to your Ladyship; nor can I have any doubt that the feelings with which you receive the tribute will be of the same mingled and saddened tone. To you, who though but little beyond the season of childhood, when the earlier numbers of this work appeared, lent the aid of your beautiful voice, and, even then, exquisite feeling for music, to the happy circle who met, to sing them together, under your father's roof, the gratification, whatever it may be, which this humble offering brings, cannot be otherwise than darkened by the mournful reflection, how many of the voices which then joined with ours are now silent in death!

PREFATORY NOTICES.

I am not without hope that, as far as regards the grace and spirit of the Melodies, you will find this closing portion of the work not unworthy of what has preceded it. The Sixteen Airs, of which the Number and the Supplement consist, have been selected from the immense mass of Irish music which has been for years past accumulating in my hands; and it was from a desire to include all that appeared most worthy of preservation, that the four supplementary songs which follow this Tenth Number have been added.

Trusting that I may yet again, in remembrance of old times, hear our voices together in some of the harmonized airs of this Volume, I have the honour to subscribe myself,

Your Ladyship's faithful Friend and Servant,

THOMAS MOORE.

Sloperton Cottage,
  May, 1834.

NOTES.

Note 1. page 7.
One chord from that harp, or one lock from that hair.

"In the twenty-eighth year of the reign of Henry VIII. an Act was made respecting the habits, and dress in general, of the Irish, whereby all persons were restrained from being shorn or shaven above the ears, or from wearing Glibbes, or *Coulins* (long locks), on their heads, or hair on their upper lip, called Crommeal. On this occasion a song was written by one of our bards, in which an Irish virgin is made to give the preference to her dear *Coulin* (or the youth with the flowing locks) to all strangers (by which the English were meant), or those who wore their habits. Of this song the air alone has reached us, and is universally admired." — Walker's *Historical Memoirs of Irish Bards*, p. 134. Mr. Walker informs us, also, that about the same period there were some harsh measures taken against the Irish Minstrels.

Note 2. page 8.
REMEMBER THE GLORIES OF BRIEN THE BRAVE.

Brien Borombe, the great Monarch of Ireland, who was killed at the battle of Clontarf, in the beginning of the 11th century, after having defeated the Danes in twenty-five engagements.

IRISH MELODIES.

NOTE 3. page 8.
Tho' lost to MONONIA *and cold in the grave.*
Munster.

NOTE 4. page 8.
He returns to KINKORA *no more!*
The palace of Brien.

NOTE 5. page 10.
Forget not our wounded companions, who stood.

This alludes to an interesting circumstance related of the Dalgais, the favourite troops of Brien, when they were interrupted in their return from the battle of Clontarf, by Fitzpatrick, prince of Ossory. The wounded men entreated that they might be allowed to fight with the rest. — " *Let stakes* (they said) *be stuck in the ground, and suffer each of us, tied to and supported by one of these stakes, to be placed in his rank by the side of a sound man.*" " Between seven and eight hundred wounded men (adds O'Halloran), pale, emaciated, and supported in this manner, appeared mixed with the foremost of the troops; — never was such another sight exhibited."— *History of Ireland*, Book XII. Chap. i.

NOTE 6. page 11.
In times of old through AMMON's *shade.*
Solis Fons, near the Temple of Ammon.

NOTES.

NOTE 7. page 16.

THE MEETING OF THE WATERS.

"The Meeting of the Waters" forms a part of that beautiful scenery which lies between Rathdrum and Arklow, in the county of Wicklow; and these lines were suggested by a visit to this romantic spot, in the summer of the year 1807.

NOTE 8. page 16.

As that vale in whose bosom the bright waters meet.

The rivers Avon and Avoca.

NOTE 9. page 19.

RICH AND RARE WERE THE GEMS SHE WORE.

This ballad is founded upon the following anecdote:—"The people were inspired with such a spirit of honour, virtue, and religion, by the great example of Brien, and by his excellent administration, that, as a proof of it, we are informed that a young lady of great beauty, adorned with jewels and a costly dress, undertook a journey alone, from one end of the kingdom to the other, with a wand only in her hand, at the top of which was a ring of exceeding great value; and such an impression had the laws and government of this monarch made on the minds of all the people, that no attempt was made upon her honour, nor was she robbed of her clothes or jewels."—WARNER's *History of Ireland*, Vol. I. Book x.

IRISH MELODIES.

Note 10. page 21.
We're fallen upon gloomy days.

I have endeavoured here, without losing that Irish character which it is my object to preserve throughout this work, to allude to the sad and ominous fatality, by which England has been deprived of so many great and good men, at a moment when she most requires all the aids of talent and integrity.

Note 11. page 22.
Thou, of the Hundred Fights!

This designation, which has been applied to Lord Nelson before, is the title given to a celebrated Irish Hero, in a Poem by O'Guive, the bard of O'Niel, which is quoted in the "Philosophical Survey of the South of Ireland," p. 433. "Con, of the hundred Fights, sleep in thy grass-grown tomb, and upbraid not our defeats with thy victories!"

Note 12. page 22.
Truth, peace, and freedom hung!

Fox, "Romanorum ultimus."

Note 13. page 25.
Where weary travellers love to call.

"In every house was one or two harps, free to all travellers, who were the more caressed the more they excelled in music."—O'Halloran.

NOTES.

Note 14.   page 29.
ST. SENANUS.

In a metrical life of St. Senanus, which is taken from an old Kilkenny MS., and may be found among the *Acta Sanctorum Hiberniæ*, we are told of his flight to the island of Scattery, and his resolution not to admit any woman of the party; he refused to receive even a sister saint, St. Cannera, whom an angel had taken to the island for the express purpose of introducing her to him. The following was the ungracious answer of Senanus, according to his poetical biographer:—

> *Cui Præsul, quid fœminis*
> *Commune est cum monachis?*
> *Nec te nec ullam aliam*
> *Admittemus in insulam.*

See the ACTA SANCT. HIB. p. 610.

According to Dr. Ledwich, St. Senanus was no less a personage than the river Shannon; but O'Connor and other antiquarians deny the metamorphose indignantly.

NOTE 15.   page 38.
When MALACHI *wore the collar of gold.*

"This brought on an encounter between Malachi (the Monarch of Ireland in the tenth century) and the Danes, in which Malachi defeated two of their champions, whom he encountered successively, hand to hand, taking a collar of gold from the neck of one, and carrying off the sword of the other, as trophies of his victory."—WARNER's *History of Ireland*, Vol. I. Book ix.

IRISH MELODIES.

NOTE 16. page 38.
Led the Red-Branch Knights to danger.

" Military orders of knights were very early established in Ireland; long before the birth of Christ we find an hereditary order of Chivalry in Ulster, called *Curaidhe na Craiobhe ruadh*, or the Knights of the Red-Branch, from their chief seat in Emania, adjoining to the palace of the Ulster kings, called *Teagh na Craiobhe ruadh*, or the Academy of the Red-Branch; and contiguous to which was a large hospital, founded for the sick knights and soldiers, called *Bronbhearg*, or the House of the Sorrowful Soldier."—O'HALLORAN's *Introduction, &c.*, Part I. Chap. v.

NOTE 17. page 38.
For the long-faded glories they cover.

It was an old tradition, in the time of Giraldus, that Lough Neagh had been originally a fountain, by whose sudden overflowing the country was inundated, and a whole region, like the Atlantis of Plato, overwhelmed. He says that the fishermen, in clear weather, used to point out to strangers the tall ecclesiastical towers under the water. *Piscatores aquæ illius turres ecclesiasticas, quæ more patriæ arctæ sunt et altæ, necnon et rotundæ, sub undis manifeste sereno tempore conspiciunt, et extraneis transeuntibus, reique causas admirantibus, frequenter ostendunt.*—TOPOGR. HIB., Dist. ii. c. 9.

NOTE 18. page 39.
THE SONG OF FIONNUALA.

To make this story intelligible in a song would require a much greater number of verses than any one is authorised to inflict upon an audience

NOTES.

at once; the reader must therefore be content to learn, in a note, that Fionnuala, the daughter of Lir, was, by some supernatural power, transformed into a swan, and condemned to wander for many hundred years, over certain lakes and rivers in Ireland, till the coming of Christianity, when the first sound of the mass-bell was to be the signal of her release. —I found this fanciful fiction among some manuscript translations from the Irish, which were begun under the direction of that enlightened friend of Ireland, the late Countess of Moira.

NOTE 19. page 43.

Like the bright lamp, that shone in KILDARE's holy fane.

The inextinguishable fire of St. Bridget, at Kildare, which Giraldus mentions, "Apud Kildariam occurrit Ignis Sanctæ Brigidæ, quem inextinguibilem vocant; non quod extingui non possit, sed quod tam solicite moniales et sanctæ mulieres ignem, suppetente materia, fovent et nutriunt, ut a tempore virginis per tot annorum curricula semper mansit inextinctus."—*Girald. Camb. de Mirabil. Hibern.*, Dist. ii. c. 34.

NOTE 20. page 44.

And daylight and liberty bless the young flower.

Mrs. H. Tighe, in her exquisite lines on the lily, has applied this image to a still more important object.

NOTE 21. page 45.

OH! BLAME NOT THE BARD.

We may suppose this apology to have been uttered by one of those wandering bards, whom Spenser so severely, and perhaps truly, describes in his "State of Ireland," and whose poems, he tells us, "were sprinkled

IRISH MELODIES.

with some pretty flowers of their natural device, which have good grace and comeliness unto them, the which it is great pity to see abused to the gracing of wickedness and vice, which, with good usage, would serve to adorn and beautify virtue."

NOTE 22. page 45.
Might have bent a proud bow to the warrior's dart.

It is conjectured, by Wormius, that the name of Ireland is derived from *Yr*, the Runic for a *bow*, in the use of which weapon the Irish were once very expert. This derivation is certainly more creditable to us than the following : " So that Ireland (called the land of *Ire*, from the constant broils therein for 400 years) was now become the land of concord." —LLOYD'S STATE WORTHIES, art. *The Lord Grandison.*

NOTE 23. page 46.
Like the wreath of HARMODIUS, *should cover his sword.*

See the Hymn, attributed to Alcæus, Εν μυρτου κλαδι το ξιφος φορησω — "I will carry my sword, hidden in myrtles, like Harmodius and Aristogiton," &c.

NOTE 24. page 50.
Which near our planet smiling came.

"Of such celestial bodies as are visible, the sun excepted, the single moon, as despicable as it is in comparison to most of the others, is much more beneficial than they all put together."—WHISTON's *Theory, &c.*

In the *Entretiens d'Ariste,* among other ingenious emblems, we find a starry sky without a moon, with these words, *Non mille, quod absens.*

NOTES.

Note 25. page 51.
"*The brook can see no moon but this.*"

This image was suggested by the following thought, which occurs somewhere in Sir William Jones's works: "The moon looks upon many night-flowers, the night-flower sees but one moon."

Note 26. page 52.
A butterfly fresh from the night-flower's kisses.
An emblem of the soul.

Note 27. page 55.
May we pledge that horn in triumph round!

"The Irish Corna was not entirely devoted to martial purposes. In the heroic ages our ancestors quaffed Meadh out of them, as the Danish hunters do their beverage at this day."—WALKER.

Note 28. page 58.
THE IRISH PEASANT TO HIS MISTRESS.
Meaning, allegorically, the ancient church of Ireland.

Note 29. page 59.
Where shineth thy spirit, there liberty shineth too!

"Where the spirit of the Lord is, there is liberty."—St. PAUL, 2 Cor. iii. 17.

IRISH MELODIES.

Note 30. page 63.
The cold chain of Silence had hung o'er thee long.

In that rebellious but beautiful song, "When Erin first rose," there is, if I recollect right, the following line:—

"The dark chain of Silence was thrown o'er the deep."

The Chain of Silence was a sort of practical figure of rhetoric among the ancient Irish. Walker tells us of "a celebrated contention for precedence between Finn and Gaul, near Finn's palace at Almhaim, where the attending bards, anxious, if possible, to produce a cessation of hostilities, shook the Chain of Silence, and flung themselves among the ranks." See also the *Ode to Gaul, the Son of Morni, in* Miss Brooke's *Reliques of Irish Poetry.*

Note 31. page 66.
THE PRINCE'S DAY.

This song was written for a fête in honour of the Prince of Wales's birthday, given by my friend, Major Bryan, at his seat in the county of Kilkenny.

Note 32. page 71.
BY THAT LAKE, WHOSE GLOOMY SHORE.

This ballad is founded upon one of the many stories related of St. Kevin, whose bed in the rock is to be seen at Glendalough, a most gloomy and romantic spot in the county of Wicklow.

Note 33. page 71.
Sky-lark never warbles o'er.

There are many other curious traditions concerning this Lake, which may be found in Giraldus, Colgan, &c.

NOTES.

Note 34. page 74.

IT IS NOT THE TEAR AT THIS MOMENT SHED.

These lines were occasioned by the loss of a very near and dear relative, who died lately at Madeira.

Note 35. page 76.

Than to remember thee, Mary!

I have here made a feeble effort to imitate that exquisite inscription of Shenstone's, "Heu! quanto minus est cum reliquis versari quam tui meminisse!"

Note 36. page 78.

Avenging and bright fall the swift sword of Erin.

The words of this song were suggested by the very ancient Irish story called "Deirdri, or the Lamentable Fate of the Sons of Usnach," which has been translated literally from the Gaelic, by Mr. O'Flanagan (see Vol. I. of *Transactions of the Gaelic Society of Dublin*), and upon which it appears that the "Darthula of Macpherson" is founded. The treachery of Conor, King of Ulster, in putting to death the three sons of Osna, was the cause of a desolating war against Ulster, which terminated in the destruction of Eman. "This story (says Mr. O'Flanagan) has been, from time immemorial, held in high repute as one of the three tragic stories of the Irish. These are, 'The death of the children of Touran;' 'The death of the children of Lear' (both regarding Tuatha de Danans); and this, 'The death of the children of Usnach,' which is a Milesian story." It will be recollected that, in the Second Number of these Melodies, there is a ballad upon the story of the children of Lear or Lir; "Silent, oh Moyle!" &c.

IRISH MELODIES.

Whatever may be thought of those sanguine claims to antiquity, which Mr. O'FLANAGAN and others advance for the literature of Ireland, it would be a very lasting reproach upon our nationality, if the Gaelic researches of this gentleman did not meet with all the liberal encouragement they merit.

NOTE 37. page 78.
By the red cloud that hung over CONOR'*s dark dwelling.*
"Oh Nasi! view that cloud that I here see in the sky! I see over Eman-green a chilling cloud of blood-tinged red."—*Deidris Song.*

NOTE 38. page 78.
When ULAD'*s three champions lay sleeping in gore.*
Ulster.

NOTE 39. page 83.
I think, oh my love! 'tis thy voice from the kingdom of souls.
"There are countries," says MONTAIGNE, "where they believe the souls of the happy live in all manner of liberty, in delightful fields; and that it is those souls, repeating the words we utter which we call Echo."

NOTE 40. page 84.
Through MORNA'*s grove.*
" Steals silently to Morna's grove."
See a translation from the Irish, in Mr. Bunting's collection, by JOHN BROWN, one of my earliest college companions and friends; whose death was as singularly melancholy and unfortunate as his life had been amiable, honourable, and exemplary.

NOTES.

NOTE 41. page 87.
And neglected his task for the flowers on the way.
Proposito florem prætulit officio.—PROPERT. Lib. i. Eleg. 20.

NOTE 42. page 88.
A triple grass.

St. Patrick is said to have made use of that species of the trefoil, to which in Ireland we give the name of Shamrock, in explaining the doctrine of the Trinity to the Pagan Irish. I do not know if there be any other reason for our adoption of this plant as a national emblem. HOPE, among the Ancients, was sometimes represented as a beautiful child, standing upon tip-toes, and a trefoil, or three-coloured grass, in her hand.

NOTE 43. page 91.
PRINCE OF BREFFNI.

These stanzas are founded upon an event of most melancholy importance to Ireland; if, as we are told by our Irish historians, it gave England the first opportunity of profiting by our divisions and subduing us. The following are the circumstances, as related by O'Halloran:—
"The king of Leinster had long conceived a violent affection for Dearbhorgil, daughter to the king of Meath, and though she had been for some time married to O'Ruark, prince of Breffni, yet it could not restrain his passion. They carried on a private correspondence, and she informed him that O'Ruark intended soon to go on a pilgrimage (an act of piety frequent in those days), and conjured him to embrace that opportunity of conveying her from a husband she detested to a lover she adored. Mac Murchad too punctually obeyed the summons, and had the lady conveyed

IRISH MELODIES.

to his capital of Ferns."—The monarch Roderick espoused the cause of O'Ruark, while Mac Murchad fled to England, and obtained the assistance of Henry II.

"Such," adds Giraldus Cambrensis (as I find him in an old translation), "is the variable and fickle nature of woman, by whom all mischief in the world (for the most part) do happen and come, as may appear by Marcus Antonius, and by the destruction of Troy."

NOTE 44. page 93.
YOU REMEMBER ELLEN.

This ballad was suggested by a well-known and interesting story told of a certain noble family in England.

NOTE 45. page 101.
We've but to make love to the lips we are near.

I believe it is Marmontel who says, "*Quand on n'a pas ce que l'on aime, il faut aimer ce que l'on a.*"—There are so many matter-of-fact people, who take such *jeux d'esprit* as this defence of inconstancy to be the actual and genuine sentiments of him who writes them, that they compel one, in self-defence, to be as matter-of-fact as themselves, and to remind them, that Democritus was not the worse physiologist for having playfully contended that snow was black; nor Erasmus in any degree the less wise for having written an ingenious encomium of folly.

NOTE 46. page 112.
Been like our Lagenian mine.

Our Wicklow gold-mines, to which this verse alludes, deserve, I fear, but too well the character here given of them.

NOTES.

NOTE 47. page 112.

Has Hope, like the bird in the story.

" The bird, having got its prize, settled not far off, with the talisman in his mouth. The prince drew near it, hoping it would drop it; but as he approached, the bird took wing, and settled again," &c.— *Arabian Nights— Story of Kummir al Zummaun and the Princess of China.*

NOTE 48. page 120.

Like him the Sprite.

This alludes to a kind of Irish fairy, which is to be met with, they say, in the fields at dusk;—as long as you keep your eyes upon him, he is fixed, and in your power; but the moment you look away (and he is ingenious in furnishing some inducement) he vanishes. I had thought that this was the sprite which we call the Leprechaun; but a high authority upon such subjects, Lady MORGAN (in a note upon her national and interesting novel, O'Donnel), has given a very different account of that goblin.

NOTE 49. page 131.

At once, like a Sun-burst, her banner unfurl'd.

" The Sun-burst" was the fanciful name given by the ancient Irish to the royal banner.

IRISH MELODIES.

NOTE 50. page 136.
'Mid desolation tuneful still!
" Dimidio magicæ resonant ubi Memnone chordæ."—JUVENAL.

NOTE 51. page 148.
Tho' the nymphs may have livelier poets to sing them.
" Tous les habitans de Mercure sont vifs."—*Pluralité des Mondes.*

NOTE 52. page 149.
And look, in their twilights, as lovely as you.
" La Terre pourra être pour Vénus l'étoile du berger et la mère des amours, comme Vénus l'est pour nous."—*Ibid.*

NOTE 53. page 157.
Yes, sad one of SION, *if closely resembling.*
These verses were written after the perusal of a treatise by Mr. Hamilton, professing to prove that the Irish were originally Jews.

NOTE 54. page 157.
And " while it is day yet, her sun hath gone down."
" Her sun is gone down while it was yet day."—JER. xv. 9.

NOTE 55. page 158.
Ah, well may we call her like thee, " the Forsaken."
" Thou shalt no more be termed Forsaken."—ISAIAH, lxii. 4.

NOTES.

Note 56. page 158.
When that cup, which for others the proud Golden City.
" How hath the oppressor ceased! the golden city ceased!"—Isaiah, xiv. 11.

Note 57. page 158.
And, a ruin, at last, for the earth-worm to cover.
" Thy pomp is brought down to the grave . . . . . and the worms cover thee."—Isaiah, xiv. 4.

Note 58. page 158.
The Lady of Kingdoms lay low in the dust.
" Thou shalt no more be called the Lady of Kingdoms."—Isaiah, xlvii. 5.

Note 59. page 161.
Oh, ye Dead! oh, ye Dead! whom we know by the light you give.
Paul Zealand mentions that there is a mountain in some part of Ireland, where the ghosts of persons who have died in foreign lands walk about and converse with those they meet, like living people. If asked why they do not return to their homes, they say they are obliged to go to Mount Hecla, and disappear immediately.

Note 60. page 169.
I wish I was by that dim Lake.
These verses are meant to allude to that ancient haunt of superstition, called Patrick's Purgatory. " In the midst of these gloomy regions of

IRISH MELODIES.

Donegal (says Dr. Campbell) lay a lake, which was to become the mystic theatre of this fabled and intermediate state. In the lake were several islands; but one of them was dignified with that called the Mouth of Purgatory, which, during the dark ages, attracted the notice of all Christendom, and was the resort of penitents and pilgrims from almost every country in Europe."

"It was," as the same writer tells us, "one of the most dismal and dreary spots in the North, almost inaccessible, through deep glens and rugged mountains, frightful with impending rocks, and the hollow murmurs of the western winds in dark caverns, peopled only with such fantastic beings as the mind, however gay, is, from strange association, wont to appropriate to such gloomy scenes."— *Strictures on the Ecclesiastical and Literary History of Ireland.*

NOTE 61. page 175.
'TWAS ONE OF THOSE DREAMS, THAT BY MUSIC ARE BROUGHT.

Written during a visit to Lord Kenmare, at Killarney.

NOTE 62. page 178.
He hath been won down by them.

In describing the Skeligs (islands of the Barony of Forth), Dr. Keating says, "There is a certain attractive virtue in the soil which draws down all the birds that attempt to fly over it, and obliges them to light upon the rock."

NOTE 63. page 178.
Lakes, where the pearl lies hid.

"Nennius, a British writer of the ninth century, mentions the abundance of pearls in Ireland. Their princes, he says, hung them behind

NOTES.

their ears; and this we find confirmed by a present made, A.C. 1094, by Gilbert, Bishop of Limerick, to Anselm, Archbishop of Canterbury, of a considerable quantity of Irish pearls."—O'HALLORAN.

NOTE 64. page 178.
Glens, where Ocean comes.
Glengariff.

NOTE 65. page 180.
And breathe the fresh air of life's morning once more.
 Jours charmans, quand je songe à vos heureux instans,
 Je pense remonter le fleuve de mes ans ;
 Et mon cœur enchanté sur sa rive fleurie
 Respire encore l'air pur du matin de la vie.

NOTE 66. page 180.
Is all we enjoy of each other in this.
The same thought has been happily expressed by my friend Mr. Washington Irving, in his *Bracebridge Hall,* Vol. I. p. 213. The pleasure which I feel in calling this gentleman my friend, is much enhanced by the reflection that he is too good an American to have admitted me so readily to such a distinction, if he had not known that my feelings towards the great and free country that gave him birth have long been such as every real lover of the liberty and happiness of the human race must entertain.

IRISH MELODIES.

NOTE 67. page 182.
And proclaim to the world what a star hath been lost!
It is only the two first verses that are either fitted or intended to be sung.

NOTE 68. page 185.
DESMOND'S SONG.
"Thomas, the heir of the Desmond family, had accidentally been so engaged in the chase, that he was benighted near Tralee, and obliged to take shelter at the Abbey of Feal, in the house of one of his dependents, called Mac Cormac. Catherine, a beautiful daughter of his host, instantly inspired the Earl with a violent passion, which he could not subdue. He married her, and by this inferior alliance alienated his followers, whose brutal pride regarded this indulgence of his love as an unpardonable degradation of his family."—LELAND, Vol. II.

NOTE 69. page 187.
Like him, the boy, who born among.
The God of Silence, thus pictured by the Egyptians.

NOTE 70. page 193.
As from a parting spirit, came.
The thought here was suggested by some beautiful lines in Mr. Rogers's Poem of *Human Life*, beginning —
"Now in the glimmering, dying light she grows
Less and less earthly."

NOTES.

I would quote the entire passage, but that I fear to put my own humble imitation of it out of countenance.

NOTE 71. page 197.
The wine-cup is circling in Almhin's hall.

The palace of Fin Mac-Cumhal (the Fingal of Macpherson) in Leinster. It was built on the top of the hill, which has retained from thence the name of the Hill of Allen, in the County of Kildare. The Finians, or Fenii, were the celebrated National Militia of Ireland, which this chief commanded. The introduction of the Danes in the above song is an anachronism common to most of the Finian and Ossianic legends.

NOTE 72. page 198.
And the Sun-burst o'er them floated wide.

The name given to the banner of the Irish.

NOTE 73. page 203.
Thy Naïads prepare his steed for him.

The particulars of the tradition respecting O'Donohue and his White Horse may be found in Mr. Weld's Account of Killarney, or more fully detailed in Derrick's Letters. For many years after his death, the spirit of this hero is supposed to have been seen on the morning of May-day, gliding over the lake on his favourite white horse, to the sound of sweet unearthly music, and preceded by groups of youths and maidens, who flung wreaths of delicate spring-flowers in his path.

IRISH MELODIES.

Among other stories connected with this Legend of the Lakes, it is said that there was a young and beautiful girl, whose imagination was so impressed with the idea of this visionary chieftain, that she fancied herself in love with him, and at last, in a fit of insanity, on a May-morning, threw herself into the lake.

NOTE 74. page 204.
When newly launch'd, thy long mane curls.

The boatmen at Killarney call those waves which come on a windy day, crested with foam, " O'Donohue's white horses."

NOTE 75. page 209.
Was like that rock of the Druid race.

The Rocking Stones of the Druids, some of which no force is able to dislodge from their stations.

NOTE 76. page 210.
" Our destin'd home or grave?"

"Milesius remembered the remarkable prediction of the principal Druid, who foretold that the posterity of Gadelus should obtain the possession of a Western Island (which was Ireland), and there inhabit."— KEATING.

NOTES.

NOTE 77. page 210.
"'*Tis Innisfail—'tis Innisfail!*"
The Island of Destiny, one of the ancient names of Ireland.

NOTE 78. page 213.
Which dreaming poets sing.
"The inhabitants of Arranmore are still persuaded that, in a clear day, they can see from this coast Hy Brysail, or the Enchanted Island, the Paradise of the Pagan Irish, and concerning which they relate a number of romantic stories."—BEAUFORT's *Ancient Topography of Ireland.*

NOTE 79. page 215.
SILENCE IS IN OUR FESTAL HALLS.
It is hardly necessary, perhaps, to inform the reader, that these lines are meant as a tribute of sincere friendship to the memory of an old and valued colleague in this work, Sir John Stevenson.

NOTE 80. page 217.
Lay his sword by his side—it hath serv'd him too well.
It was the custom of the ancient Irish, in the manner of the Scythians, to bury the favourite swords of their heroes along with them.

INDEX.

	PAGE
ALONE in crowds to wander on	211
And doth not a meeting like this make amends	179
As a beam o'er the face of the waters may glow	18
As slow our ship her foamy track	137
As vanquish'd Erin wept beside	190
At the mid hour of night, when stars are weeping, I fly	83
Avenging and bright fall the swift sword of Erin	78
Believe me, if all those endearing young charms	36
By that Lake, whose gloomy shore	71
By the Feal's wave benighted	185
By the hope within us springing	54
Come o'er the sea	113
Come, rest in this bosom, my own stricken deer	133
Come, send round the wine, and leave points of belief	40
Dear Harp of my Country! in darkness I found thee	63

INDEX.

	PAGE
Down in the valley come meet me to-night	162
Drink of this cup;—you'll find there's a spell in	159
Drink to her who long	47
Erin! the tear and the smile in thine eyes	5
Fairest! put on awhile	177
Farewell!—but whenever you welcome the hour	103
Fill the bumper fair	122
Fly not yet, 'tis just the hour	11
Forget not the field where they perish'd	134
From this hour the pledge is given	196
Go where Glory waits thee	1
Has sorrow thy young days shaded	111
Here we dwell, in holiest bowers	76
How dear to me the hour when daylight dies	22
How oft has the Benshee cried	21
How sweet the answer Echo makes	165
I'd mourn the hopes that leave me	107
If thou'lt be mine, the treasures of air	153
In the morning of life, when its cares are unknown	139
In yonder valley there dwelt, alone	188
I saw from the beach, when the morning was shining	199
I saw thy form in youthful prime	75
I wish I was by that dim Lake	169
It is not the tear at this moment shed	74
I've a secret to tell thee, but hush! not here	187

INDEX.

	PAGE
Lay his sword by his side—it hath serv'd him too well	217
Lesbia hath a beaming eye	68
Let Erin remember the days of old	38
Like the bright lamp, that shone in Kildare's holy fane	43
My gentle Harp, once more I waken	135
Nay, tell me not, dear, that the goblet drowns	81
Ne'er ask the hour—what is it to us	151
Night clos'd around the conqueror's way	56
No, not more welcome the fairy numbers	125
Of all the fair months, that round the sun	203
Oh! Arranmore, lov'd Arranmore	212
Oh banquet not in those shining bowers	164
Oh! blame not the bard, if he flies to the bowers	45
Oh! breathe not his name, let it sleep in the shade	6
Oh! could we do with this world of ours	214
Oh! doubt me not—the season	105
Oh for the swords of former time	155
Oh! had we some bright little isle of our own	57
Oh! haste and leave this sacred isle	29
Oh! the days are gone, when Beauty bright	64
Oh, the sight entrancing	173
Oh! think not my spirits are always as light	14
Oh, ye Dead! oh, ye Dead! whom we know by the light you give	161
Oh! weep for the hour	34

INDEX.

	PAGE
Oh ! where's the slave so lowly	118
One bumper at parting !—tho' many	109
Quick ! we have but a second	168
Remember the Glories of Brien the Brave	8
Remember thee ; yes, while there's life in this heart	4
Rich and rare were the gems she wore	19
Sail on, sail on, thou fearless bark	156
Shall the Harp then be silent, when he who first gave	182
She is far from the land where her young hero sleeps	80
She sung of Love, while o'er her lyre	193
Silence is in our festal halls	215
Silent, oh Moyle ! be the roar of thy water	39
Sing — sing — Music was given	206
Sing, sweet Harp, oh sing to me	191
Strike the gay harp ! see the moon is on high	194
Sublime was the warning that Liberty spoke..	41
Sweet Innisfallen, fare thee well	171
Take back the virgin page	27
The dawning of morn, the daylight's sinking	166
The dream of those days when first I sung thee is o'er	200
The harp that once through Tara's halls	13
The Minstrel-Boy to the war is gone	99
The time I've lost in wooing	119
The valley lay smiling before me	91

INDEX.

	PAGE
The wine-cup is circling in Almhin's hall	197
The young May moon is beaming, love	84
There are sounds of mirth in the night-air ringing	208
There is not in the wide world a valley so sweet	16
They came from a land beyond the sea	210
They know not my heart, who believe there can be	128
They may rail at this life—from the hour I began it	148
This life is all chequer'd with pleasures and woes	86
Tho' dark are our sorrows, to-day we'll forget them	66
Tho' the last glimpse of Erin with sorrow I see	7
Though humble the banquet to which I invite thee	126
Through Erin's isle	88
Through grief and through danger thy smile hath cheer'd my way	58
'Tis believ'd that this Harp, which I wake now for thee	60
'Tis gone, and for ever, the light we saw breaking	131
'Tis sweet to think, that, where'er we rove	101
'Tis the last rose of summer	95
To Ladies' eyes around, boy	143
To-morrow, comrade, we	201
'Twas one of those dreams, that by music are brought	175
We may roam thro' this world, like a child at a feast	31
Weep on, weep on, your hour is past	61
What life like that of the bard can be	205
What the bee is to the floweret	79
When cold in the earth lies the friend thou hast loved	141
When daylight was yet sleeping under the billow	52

INDEX.

	PAGE
When first I met thee, warm and young	115
When he, who adores thee, has left but the name	23
When in death I shall calmly recline	24
When thro' life unblest we rove	97
Whene'er I see those smiling eyes	154
While gazing on the moon's light	50
While History's Muse the memorial was keeping	129
Wreath the bowl	145
Yes, sad one of Sion, if closely resembling	157
You remember Ellen, our hamlet's pride	93